IT CAN BE DONE

It Can Be Done

Emmanuel Adewusi

CCCG Publishing House

Contents

Copyright	vi
Dedication	vii
Preface	ix
Introduction	xi
1 The Will of God	1
2 How Will it be Done?	74
3 Hindrances to Faith	83
4 How do we Build our Faith?	88
5 Evidence of Faith	93
6 Faith in Action	96
7 Who Will do it?	101
8 When Will it be Done?	110
9 The Spirit of Faith	125
Epilogue	133
Contact the Author	135
A Sinner's Prayer	137
About the Author	139

Copyright © 2022 Emmanuel Adewusi

All rights reserved. No part of this book may be used or reproduced by any means, graphics, electronic, or mechanical, including photocopying, recording, taping, or by any information storage retrieval system without the author's written permission except in cases of brief quotations embodied in critical articles and reviews.

Scriptures are taken from New King James Version. Copyright 1979, 1980, 1982 by Thomas Nelson, Inc. Used by permission. All right reserved.

Author: Emmanuel Adewusi

ISBN: 978-1-989099-12-4 (hardcover)
ISBN: 978-1-989099-13-1 (ebook)

First Printing 2022

Dedication

To all those who want to believe in God more today than ever.

To all those who want the faith of Abraham but with the grace that Jesus Christ came to offer.

To all those who desire to do greater works than Jesus Christ ever did.

To all those who know that they are still scratching the surface of what they can do for God.

To all those who want to see every promise Jesus Christ made to them come to pass.

Yes! YOU! This book is dedicated to YOU!

Preface

One thing that amazes me about our Heavenly Father, is His concept of what can or cannot be done. We often have difficulty relating with Him because we cannot accurately translate His Word into our reality. God said in Isaiah 55:8-9, *"For My thoughts are not your thoughts, nor are your ways My ways," says the Lord. "For as the heavens are higher than the earth, so are My ways higher than your ways, and My thoughts than your thoughts."* We will always struggle to believe in God until we realize that we can only relate with Him from our spirit and not our minds. This is why faith is needed to please God (Hebrews 11:6). Understanding is to the mind as faith is to the human spirit.

It is a sign of pride to suggest that we can understand God with our mental faculties. God speaks from His own reality, so it is impossible to walk in agreement with Him until we exist in His reality. A key question is asked in Amos 3:3, *"Can two walk together, unless they are agreed?"* The simple answer is no! Faith is the glue that helps us walk in agreement with God. Faith allows us to take steps based on what God says, even when we do not mentally comprehend it.

The title of this book is prophetic. When you finish reading this book, your response to everything God tells you to do will be, *"It Can be Done!"*

Introduction

During the early stages of Cornerstone Christian Church of God, God began speaking to me about finding a church building to call our own. At that time, we were renting a space for our services on Sundays, Thursdays and every last Friday of the month, with the children's church finding its home in the kitchen. God's intention for this instruction was for us to begin to save as much money as possible for the down payment of our future church building. And since God is a God of order, His instructions were specific concerning our approach. My natural mind struggled to understand how the financial aspect would come together because, at the time, we had about 20-25 members consistently attending the church. However, I did not allow it to hinder me, and so our faith journey began.

We were first tasked with hiring a realtor and started our search for a property. We came across many options with listing prices that would shock anyone buying a church property for the first time. Although the high prices posed a challenge, I did not allow this to distract me from the direction God was moving in. God had spoken, and all we needed to do was move accordingly.

As our journey continued, we found a building that met our criteria and submitted an offer, but it was rejected. I later found out that our offer was one of the lowest bids for the property. As our search progressed, the listing prices we saw increased, but so did my faith as I remained steadfast and believed in God's promise. I always say, "If God cannot do it, then let it be undone."

God, being so faithful, exceeded our expectations. We eventually found the right building, which was priced at over $1,000,000 CAD. Something about one million dollars can make a person cringe if they do not have faith—we are talking about six zeros! But since I had built my faith from the moment we began our property search, I was, surprisingly, unconcerned about the numbers by this time.

You see, faith is like a ladder - you can move from one level to the next. As you climb up this ladder, you will be able to look back in amazement as you face life's challenges with ease. In the same way, bodybuilders gain muscle, you can also intentionally spend time building your faith.

This world is built on the Law of Exchange, which I've had the privilege to preach on and encourage you to locate online because I know it will be a huge blessing to you. This Law of Exchange simply means that anything of value can be created or brought into existence if you have the right things to exchange for it. We can understand this principle from a commerce perspective, where we exchange money for a product or service. We measure the value of a thing by the amount of money we pay to receive that product or service. We can exchange everything we desire for something God has freely given to another person. What you will learn in this book will effectively erase the need to envy anyone. You will know how to get whatever you desire, especially what God desires for you. Are you ready for it?

Allow me to take you back to the beginning for a moment, to Genesis 1, when our Father in heaven, the master creator, was reversing the dire situation on the earth, to be exact. He followed some key steps:

1. **The Holy Spirit was hovering over the face of the deep.**
2. **God declared what He wanted to see.**
3. **God put His hands to work.**

Every human being can relate their lives with the hopelessness of the situation on the earth in the beginning. In the beginning, the earth was nothing to write home about. God, however, made specific declarations and got to work on transforming the earth into a sight to behold. The steps God took in Genesis 1 are a clear picture of what the Law of Exchange is all about. The Law of Attraction is similar to the Law of Exchange but with one critical difference: the role of the spirit in creating your desires. The Law of Attraction simply states that whatever you desire and declare will be attracted to you. To create anything over time, all you need is the stirring of the spirit (positively or negatively), the spoken word of what your heart truly desires, and the action that aligns with what your heart desires. My issue with the mainstream version of the Law of Attraction is that it does not account for the Holy Spirit's role in directing the extent of what we create. The extent of what we create is our responsibility, but the Holy Spirit has been given to the children of God to enable us to create the right things (Romans 8:26-27).

To apply the principles of the law of exchange consistently and not give up, you need to operate more in the future instead of the past or present. Faith enables us to operate more in the realm of what can be (the future) as opposed to what has been (the past) or what is (the present). Faith is a choice in the same way doubt is a choice. When God gives a word, and we respond in the affirmative, we operate in faith and come into agreement with God. Like a signature on a contract, our faith response is what activates a promise and sets it in motion.

There is no need for evidence when faith is present because faith is the evidence. Hallelujah! This response of faith is what invites God's presence into a situation. He is ever pleased with faith. This book serves as a guide for you to build your faith as you work towards doing and becoming all that God has called you to do and become. Ecclesiastes 10:15 tells us that *"fools are so exhausted by a little work that they can't even find their way home."* This book will enable you to take the right steps towards faith-building so you can hit every one of your God-given targets.

God's faithfulness cannot be compared to anything I have ever experienced because He continuously exceeds my expectations. Not only did God provide for the building, but He also sent the resources for the renovation project, which kicked off immediately after purchasing the building. We spent over $500,000 CAD on renovations alone. Many years ago, that amount alone would have previously caused me stress. Now, I could not have been more at peace. I watched in awe as resources came from around the world to complete the work of God.

Here are some pictures of the building during and after renovations:

Children's Church | Preschool

Introduction | *xv*

Main Sanctuary

Main Sanctuary

Main Sanctuary

Main Sanctuary

Main Sanctuary

Men's Washroom

Main Sanctuary | Before

Main Sanctuary | After

Introduction | *xix*

Main Sanctuary

Main Sanctuary

Front Entrance | Lobby

Faith Room

Upstairs Hallway

Upstairs Hallway

As you continue reading, I want you to keep a question in the back of your mind. When God gives you a picture of His plans for you, will your heart say yes to it? As we discuss faith, I hope your faith will grow to the point where you can enthusiastically respond to my question. Enjoy the journey!

1

The Will of God

The pursuit of purpose is an effective driver of faith, so knowing the will of God is therefore essential to building faith. You cannot build faith without working towards a purpose. We build our faith to have the capacity to say yes to the will of God; because faith in Him allows us to move when He says to move and stop when He says to stop. Moses needed to have faith to lead the children of Israel after God instructed them to move forward in the direction of the Red Sea. (Exodus 14:15-23). Without a knowledge of God's purpose for bringing the Israelites out of bondage, it would've been more difficult to obey God faithfully. Since Moses knew and accepted the will of God for the children of Israel, he had faith to carry out the assignment of leading them into the Promised Land.

The will of God is what God plans to happen. In teaching us how to pray, Jesus said, *"Your kingdom come. Your will be done on earth as it is in heaven."* (Matthew 6:10). God has always had a will for His creation; remember, He did not give up on us in the garden. His thoughts for us are still good, and His plans remain for a bright future.

Just like we, as humans, have our own will, God also has a will. When Jesus Christ was nearing the end of His earthly ministry and dying on the cross seemed difficult to do, He prayed, *"Father, if it is Your Will, take this cup away from Me; nevertheless not My will, but Yours, be done."* (Luke 22:42). God's will is based on the plan He desires to have done in the world.

Although the will of God does not exist to massage our ego, we still gain from it coming to pass. In a sense, the will of God has nothing to do with us because it is much bigger than you and me, but it also has everything to do with us because God has made us a part of His grand plans. God said in Jeremiah 29:11 that His plans for us are of good and not evil. I once heard a minister say that his understanding of the meaning of "devil" is "a doer of evil." So, therefore, God's plan will bring good to us, while the devil's plan will bring evil.

In some cases, the Bible makes known the will of God for certain aspects of our lives. For example, the Bible clearly tells us God's will concerning our health, wealth, and marriage. We should not be in doubt as to whether God wants us to enjoy good health or not. In other cases, the will of God is made known generically, so a specific word from God is still needed to confirm God's will for each of us individually. For example, the Bible tells us that the will of God is for a man and woman to be equally yoked in a relationship, but the Bible will not specifically confirm if a woman is to marry Tom or Tunde, or if a man is to marry Susan or Sade. In essence, the will of God is known by searching scriptures and through the guidance of the Holy Spirit. Knowing the will of God is crucial to the development of our faith. The Bible tells us in Ephesians 5:17, *"Therefore do not be unwise, but understand what the will of the Lord is."*

I have seen well-meaning Christians apply their faith blindly, expecting God to "just do it", and end up disappointed and discouraged.

Some people even blame God for failing to realize their faith expectations and say, "Why didn't God correct me when I was misapplying my faith?" God puts the responsibility on Christians to find out His will, so we have to put in the work to be sure instead of assuming the will of God.

"Study to shew thyself approved unto God, a workman that needeth not to be ashamed, rightly dividing the word of truth." (2 Timothy 2:15)

Like the Bereans in Acts 17, we are to diligently study scriptures to determine God's will concerning every aspect of our lives in order to live a successful Christian life. The will of God for our salvation, baptism in the Holy Spirit, health, marriage, and finances can all be found in the Bible and can be found either by searching it or through the teachings of God's anointed ministers, who speak the word of God.

There are times in scripture when the will of God is clearly stated. At other times, it is declared after a miraculous event has occurred. To be specific, there were times when God's messengers indicated that they were acting based on God's instructions, while at other times, they did not state that, but it was made known later.

Elijah was introduced to us in 1 Kings 17:1, with the bold statement he made, *"And Elijah the Tishbite, of the inhabitants of Gilead, said to Ahab, 'As the Lord God of Israel lives, before whom I stand, there shall not be dew nor rain these years, except at my word.'"* From this passage, Elijah came up with the idea that drought was the punishment the people needed to repent. However, in 1 Kings 18:36, Elijah made it known that God ordered the drought and everything else, not him.

"And it came to pass, at the time of the offering of the evening sacrifice, that Elijah the prophet came near and said, "Lord God of Abraham, Isaac, and

Israel, let it be known this day that You are God in Israel and I am Your servant, and that I have done all these things at Your word."

It is clear from the Bible that Jesus Christ performed many miracles. Like with Elijah, we may be led to believe that Jesus did whatever He felt like doing because He had the power. This belief would be an error. Jesus, Himself said in John 5:30, *"I can of Myself do nothing. As I hear, I judge; and My judgment is righteous because I do not seek My own will but the will of the Father who sent Me."* Do you agree that we sometimes operate opposite to how Jesus did? The moment some Christians feel empowered, they do whatever they feel like doing and only consult God when they do not get the expected result. But you would be grossly mistaken to assume that you can just come up with an idea, apply your faith to it and it will come to pass. Many Christians make this mistake and end up destabilizing and paralyzing their faith. They try out their faith with whatever comes to mind, and when it does not come to pass, they are too disappointed and discouraged to try again.

In teaching us about spiritual gifts, Apostle Paul made a profound statement. After listing the different manifestations of the Holy Spirit, he said in 1 Corinthians 12:11, *"But one and the same Spirit works all these things, distributing to each one individually as He wills."* Again, we see that God has a will, and if we submit ourselves to Him, He will operate freely through us to bring about His will. When God makes His will known to you, and you can believe it and act accordingly, nothing can stop it from coming to pass. Then, we can read Mark 9:23 with confidence, which says, *"Jesus said to him, 'If you can believe, all things God says will be done are possible to him who believes.'"*

God makes His will known to us through His written and revealed word. In other words, you can know God's will by reading the Bible and paying attention to what He reveals to you, both directly and through His messengers. The will of God can be revealed through supernatural occurrences like dreams, visions, and angelic visitations; and can also be revealed through the perception of the heart or discernment. For some people, perception may sometimes be confusing, as these revelations may feel like mere manifestations of their thoughts. One of the major differences between your thoughts and the thoughts God communicates to you is that His thoughts come with joy and peace. Consider this the heavenly seal. It is like a distinct stamp that shows the origin of the mail received.

There are times, though, that you do not get the will of God directly from the word, so you have to ask God in Jesus' name. In this case, you should ask questions directly in prayer, addressed to the "Holy Spirit" because He has the information you need.

We will explore seemingly impossible situations that eventually came to be because they were the will of God. You may be wondering, "What about the scripture that says God grants us the desires of our hearts?" Yes, God does grant us the desires of our hearts, but not at the expense of His plans and purpose. It is written in Lamentations 3:37, *"Who is he who speaks and it comes to pass when the Lord has not commanded it?"* God grants the desires of our hearts when it is not at odds with His plans and purpose. God asserted in Isaiah 46:10, *"My counsel shall stand, and I will do all My pleasure."* Our faith will be strengthened when we accurately differentiate between God's will and our desires, and the expectations we ought to have in those different circumstances. The biblical accounts we explore will establish that it is only the will of God that we can confidently say will come to pass, come what may.

God's Will Concerning Your Life

I will attempt to share some perspectives concerning different areas where you may have desires and expectations from God. Our understanding of our responsibilities versus God's will enable us to receive our desires from God sooner rather than later and exercise our faith.

HEALING

Healing is a fundamental desire of man. No matter their gender, social class or race, every human being will need healing at some point in their lifetime. Multiple efforts are underway to eradicate illnesses considered to be a danger to humanity, such as the race to find a cure for cancer. The number of resources devoted to curing cancer can amount to billions of dollars. Combined, the industries that cater directly or indirectly to human health and wellness are a multi-trillion dollar industry.

The billion-dollar question though is, "What is God's will concerning my healing?" God's will concerning the health of His children is very clear. He wants us to enjoy good health all the days of our lives. In odd cases where we fall sick, He has made provisions for our healing.

Did you know that Jesus dealt with the issue of health and healing more than anything else during His earthly ministry? We see this numerous times in scripture.

"How God anointed Jesus of Nazareth with the Holy Spirit and with power, who went about doing good and healing all who were oppressed by the devil, for God was with Him" (Acts 10:38).

"When Jesus went out, He saw a great multitude, was moved with compassion for them, and healed their sick" (Matthew 14:14).

Has Jesus changed? The answer is no. It is written in Hebrews 13:8, *"Jesus Christ is the same yesterday, today, and forever."* If He was concerned with people's health then, He still is now.

If you desire healing for yourself or a loved one, know it can be done. In fact, it has already been done. It is written in 1 Peter 2:24, *"...by whose stripes you were healed."*

To partake in any scriptural provision, we must start from the end and work backwards to the beginning. What do I mean? You must see yourself already possessing what you desire before you even begin doing what needs to be done. Do you believe that sickness and disease can be healed? That is your starting point. God's part has been taken care of already. Jesus said, *"Therefore I say to you, whatever things you ask when you pray, believe that you receive them, and you will have them"* (Mark 11:24).

God has demonstrated His healing powers through many of His children in modern times. Miracles, signs, and wonders of healing are still happening today, which means that it can also happen to you. At Cornerstone, we have been privileged to see the hand of God supernaturally heal people. Here are some healing testimonies that can help build your faith for your healing.

Karla G. celebrates the healing of her lower back!

Once again, my lower back was in severe pain, and it was very difficult for me to sit, walk, or turn without discomfort. I would toss and turn while sitting, and I could not cross my legs either because it felt as if my right leg was paralyzed. I tried to cross my legs while standing, but it was still painful. One Saturday night, after cleaning the church, the cleaning team gathered to pray. It was during this prayer, the Lord used one of my lovely sisters in Christ to heal me. As she prayed for me, I felt a breeze inside my lower back. The feeling of this breeze was amazingly beautiful; words cannot describe the feeling. Since that day, I have had NO MORE LOWER BACK PAIN! I can sit without having to toss and turn and I can cross my legs. I am forever grateful to my

Heavenly Father for not just healing me but for the many, many healing testimonies that will come. I know my testimony will be a blessing to many. In Jesus' name, amen! Hallelujah.

Sunshine S. celebrates healing from substance addiction!

I have been free of drugs, alcohol, and cigarettes for 77 days!! To God be the glory. These are things that I never imagined I could be free from. I had hit rock bottom, and one time I had prayed when I was very high. I never thought the Lord would hear or help me, but He came through in a huge way! I don't have any cravings for anything whatsoever and NO WITHDRAWALS. Thank you big time, Lord. And I'd like to thank the Lord for giving me Cornerstone as my family and support; I appreciate you guys. Lord, you have restored and transformed me. Everyone sees a difference, and I am forever grateful.

We followed up with Sunshine, and she sent her love. At the time of publishing this book, Sunshine has now celebrated 1 year of sobriety from drugs, alcohol, and cigarettes. She writes, "Glory be to God!"

Ifeoma O. celebrates the healing of her spinal cord!

I thank God for healing me. In the last week of May, I suddenly started experiencing severe pain around my spinal cord, precisely where I was given an epidural during the birth of my son one year ago. The pain was so severe that sitting was painful. Laying on my back would bring me to tears. On June 3rd, during one of our bible study services, I asked God to take away the pain as I partook in the Holy Communion. I expected instant healing, but nothing happened. Still, I chose not to focus on the pain. By the next day, the pain was gone.

Jason D. celebrates the healing of his heart!

Last December, I was admitted to the cardiac ward at the Royal Alexandra Hospital. I was diagnosed with congestive heart failure and given 1-2 years to live. They told me a normal heart operates at 50%-60% capacity. Mine was at 15%.

I went for another test on my heart, and by April 20th, I received a call from the hospital. The lady told me, in her words, "In 20 years, I have never seen anything like this." My heart is not only back to normal; it is at 69%. One person asked me today, "What did you do to get better?" I replied, "I could not do anything to help the situation. Diet and exercise were irrelevant at this point. God healed me."

Although it was difficult at times to keep the faith, it was by faith alone that I am here now. By God's grace, I will be here for a very long time. God put me to work in my two weeks in the hospital. I spoke the Word to the ones that needed to hear it, even though my faith was wavering and my confidence was growing weak. I did not know if my last task on earth was to speak the Word to one last person before I died, but I refused to give in.

Some people ask to see real evidence of God. They don't understand that evidence belongs to the individual. That is to say, God gives evidence to each one of us and only for that person.

This is my testimony and this is real evidence, documented by the hospital, of the miracles of God. I am very far from perfect, but I gave my life to our living God, and I will not turn my back on my Lord.

Sola O. celebrates the healing of his back!

I want to praise God for His healing power in this movement. I woke up one Wednesday morning with back pain shooting down my right leg. The pain was so bad it took me about 5-7 seconds before I could stand upright. This pain persisted throughout the day, and nothing I did resolved it.

The next day was the first day of the month, and I was unable to attend the bible studies and communion service in person so my family and I decided to stream the service from home. While the service was going on it was time for the communion, so I took a cup of orange juice and a cracker to join the communion, and upon the pastor's advice, I prayed for something I wanted. I placed my hand on my lower back and prayed to God. I prayed and asked God to heal me of my back pain and said that by Sunday, I did not want to feel the pain again.

Of course, by the next day, Friday, the pain intensified, but my faith in Jesus was stronger. At some point, I could not sit down to work, and I had to lay on the bed to relieve some of the pain. My wife jumped on my back when she saw me lying down, and I asked her to get off. She said, "don't you have faith that your back pain will go away?" I replied that I believe by faith that my back pain is gone; however, I still feel some pain right now. The day went on, and the pain was still there, but I held on to my faith and didn't pay attention to it.

By Saturday morning, I felt the very first sign of relief, and I began to praise God for my healing. As the day went on, the pain dissipated even more, and by Sunday morning, it was totally gone. I give God all the praise for my healing.

Olamide O. celebrates the healing of her digestive system!

I would like to give thanks to God for divine healing. Sometime in February 2021, I began experiencing minor diarrhea, which didn't seem like a big deal. I decided to go to bed, and I felt the urge to use the bathroom in the middle of the night. I realized something wasn't right as I saw some excreta in the wrong area. I went to bed and then realized my sheets were stained.

The next day, I went to the emergency room, and after hours and hours of waiting, I began praying under my breath and finally, I was taken in for a physical examination. I was later told the issue could be what they call a "rectovaginal fistula."

Over the weeks, I went through various physical examinations: MRI, CT scan, and colonoscopy, and each test result came back with perfect results. This was indeed a miracle because the doctors were confused and had no explanation for the test results that came back perfect. I just want to thank God, who is the almighty physician, for His faithfulness and healing.

Victor O. celebrates the restoration of his health!

I want to thank God for restoring my health. My physical body was attacked with a cold, fever, headache, and body pains. Initially, I engaged in prayer for healing; consequently, to no avail, the situation intensified. When I got to my wits' end in faith, I decided to escalate to my spiritual father. Though I did not get him on the phone, the cold and fever left immediately when I put down the phone, and the other symptoms alleviated immediately. Later, when my spiritual father returned my call, he corrected me by highlighting that I was engaged in the wrong spiritual practice. I learned the attack on my health was a spiritual attack. He instructed me to rebuke the devil myself. To the glory of God, my health was restored the next day and was perfected by the end of the week.

Isatu M. celebrates the healing of her physical body!

Good morning Church! I thank God for healing me at the Come & See: Healing & Deliverance Conference. I've had this pain going through my neck down to my leg from an accident that happened in 2008. This pain had been affecting me for a long time. I've had to go on short-term disability and to physiotherapy several times because of how debilitating the pain was. It got so severe that I was referred for pain treatment using injections, but I decided in my heart that I would trust God for complete healing. As the spirit of God was moving at the conference, God completely healed the pain in my neck all the way to my leg. On top of that, He also healed the pain in my throat. Now I can sing and worship without strain!

Sheila O. celebrates emotional healing!

I would like to thank God for healing and restoring me emotionally. The message on trauma helped me realize that there were experiences I thought I had successfully handled but had instead been pushed to the back of my mind. The memories of these experiences would often trigger unhealthy emotional responses in me. I had been emotionally unhealthy but did not realize it. During the message, there were many connections to what I had been through; God had me in mind and wanted to heal me. Thank God for spiritual authority; I sought help and got it. Today, I can confidently state that I have been delivered and restored. Thank you, Jesus!

Bernie G. celebrates the restoration of her health!

I want to give thanks to God for healing and restoring my health. I had a health scare in December 2019 just before Christmas. I had several doctor appointments and visits to ultrasound centres. It got to a point after the biopsy that I was referred to a surgeon. I was terrified but went to God in prayer. At each clinic visit and ultrasound, I declared healing upon myself and rejected everything they reported to me.

I reached out to Pastor Emmanuel, and he said we should agree in prayer. Pastor Emmanuel prayed with me and told me that I should call him on the day of my appointment with the surgeon. The way he said it was well with me in Jesus' Name, in a calm and subtle voice, I was like, oh my gosh, Pastor does not understand the gravity of what I am saying.

At that time, anointing oil became my second skin lotion. With faith, I prayed and made proclamations over myself.

Anyway, the day to see the surgeon came. Pastor and I prayed that morning. When I got to the appointment, she checked me, and she appeared kind of confused. She asked what I was told when I went to the ultrasound, and I told her. She then said she was sending me to another ultrasound, and this would be the third.

Three technicians, a head nurse and a doctor, came but could find nothing. They were confused. All the while I was just saying, "I am healed in the mighty name of Jesus." They gave me another appointment for six months and said my surgeon would contact me. She contacted me a week later and told me not to return for the appointment, but if I noticed or felt anything, I should contact her. All this happened from December 2019 to December 2020.

They couldn't find anything, and I'm healed in Jesus' Name.

Naharah W. celebrates the healing of her wrist!

Having pain in my wrist, I initially anointed and prayed over it myself, but when the pain remained, I asked Pastor Emmanuel to pray for healing, and now there is no pain!

Pauline J. celebrates healing from arthritis!

For the past two weeks, the fingers on my right hand were in pain, and I had problems bending the middle finger.

During one of our bible studies, Pastor Emmanuel spoke life into every bone and commanded arthritis to be gone in Jesus' Name! I received that word, and almost instantly, the pain in my fingers stopped. I am able to bend every finger without any issues. I thank God for His healing power, Hallelujah!

Iseoluwa O. celebrates healing from unbearable stomach pains that were found to be a cyst!

On December 12th, 2021, God told me to prepare this testimony.

For more than 3 years, my enemy had unbearable stomach pains that would just not go. Nothing brought it on and sometimes it would even wake me up at night. It usually started with heartburn that worked its way down into my stomach, causing me to throw up. It was like I was being stabbed repeatedly and someone was twisting everything inside of me. The doctors were confused and had varying diagnoses because of the symptoms my enemy experienced.

After a while I just didn't even bother going to the clinic or hospital anymore. It was almost like it was a part of me I had to live with and endure. Me and my family would pray and recite healing scriptures but the pain never left. I had told God "how exactly did you want me to stand in front of proclaiming you and not experience you in this dimension." After that came many attacks and no peace of mind only to distract me from God's incoming blessing. Little did I know what He had in store.

During a physical in March, the doctor found my enemy had a heart murmur of which she wasn't sure if it was benign. I requested to be referred to an obgyn and she didn't want to at first because she didn't see the need but eventually agreed after my insistence. I had an ultrasound done and they found a really big cyst.

During Come and See in April 2022, the OBGYN called while I was in church and said he was surprised with the amount of pain I had and size of the cyst, how the right ovary had not turned on itself completely and died. He gave me two options: birth control or surgery, but said he didn't recommend birth control as he doesn't think it would help at this stage. I didn't even think twice before saying I would go with the surgery. I held on to someone's testimony from that night- she had mentioned she was scheduled for a surgery earlier for which she went for but was turned back as the doctor said it was not needed anymore. I remember that night saying my healing was made permanent.

One day Pastor Emmanuel spoke about the mantle and had asked us to bring towels to pray on. Returning home, I got the inclination to put the mantle on my chest and my belly and sleep with it over my head with Divine Encounter playing on repeat. Once or twice that night I was woken up as I felt a presence and I would pray in tongues and go back to sleep. Periodically Pastor would check in and pray, and would ask if I was okay with the surgery and what my faith could carry. I would say I was fine with it and I also honestly didn't mind going to the hospital and being turned back. I was fine with however God wanted to showcase himself.

Nearing the end of April he said we should fast and pray while meditating on 1 Peter 2:24. I also started ignoring the pains and making declarations once it came.

The day before the surgery on May 23rd I woke up really happy, dancing like a crazy person. I didn't know why I was just happy. On the day of the surgery, my mum and I prayed before going through the OR. I got acquainted with the anesthesiologist and before they put me to sleep I asked if they didn't mind us praying. I just remember saying God please hold their hands. I remember waking up post-op with my mum at my side I just heard her telling someone they went in and didn't find anything. The next day I saw a note from the doctors saying:

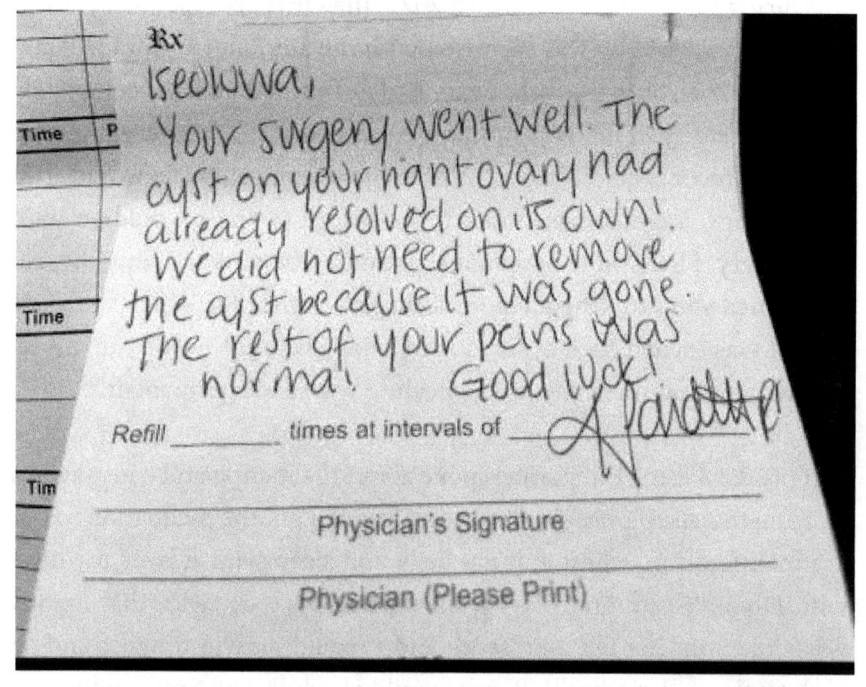

> Iseoluwa,
> Your surgery went well. The cyst on your right ovary had already resolved on its own. We did not need to remove the cyst because it was gone. The rest of your pains was normal. Good luck!

Physician's Note

I want to Thank God because he perfected my health without help from doctors and I know that it was important for them to open me up so everyone could be convinced beyond reasonable doubt that it was gone, not on its own but by the hand of God! I want to also thank God that my profession (as a nurse) didn't rob me of my testimony of having to explain His blessings away.

Leonie A. celebrates healing and protection!

Good morning church I just want to say my daughter has always invited me to night prayers, and I would tell her that I have problems driving at night. But Shimona is very persistent, so I decided to attend the last service. After service I was going to my car and I fell in the parking lot and hit my head and back. One of the members assisted me to get up and walked me to my car. It was very difficult for me to drive home, but by the grace of God and my 13 year old daughter, I was guided home as she had to tell me when I could change lanes because the pain I was having in my head restricted me from doing the shoulder check. When I got home the pain in my back and head was getting worse so I took 2 extra strength Tylenol. The pain eased a lot but came back even stronger after it wore off. I could not take the pain anymore so I decided to go to the emergency room and was there for almost 9 hrs. They took me for X-rays and an MRI, the result came back that I had a mild concussion and bruised ribs and I was given an injection for the pain and Tylenol with codeine. I had to wait until the pain subdued before I could leave the emergency, the pain was back again after the medication wore off and I had to keep taking the tablet that the doctor gave me to take home. I got up that Monday morning just bawling because the pain was unbearable. Pastor called to find out how I was doing, and after praying with me, I dozed off and I did not get up until the next day. There was a slight pain but I rebuked it in Jesus name. From that day till now there have been no pain in my back or head. I just want to give God all the praise and glory for healing me and for Pastor that prayed for my healing.

Mekelle C. celebrates the restoration of her daughter's health!

On Saturday, I got a call that when I returned home, I needed to bring something for Miesha, my daughter, because she was not her best. I made a stop at the pharmacy and got Panadol and soup. By Sunday night and early morning on Monday, she was crying from pain and discomfort with a fever of 102°. We went to the clinic and were prescribed medication. We were also told the different possibilities during this time, but I continued believing in prayer. I asked her if she believed God would heal her, and we stood in faith for healing. During this time, my Aunt called and shared some news of how she had experienced two patient deaths within two days. The Holy Spirit gave me Ezekiel 37 to prophecy concerning what seemed dead and lifeless, which I did. Miesha is now restored, and by God's grace, all is well!

Pauline J. celebrates the restoration of her son, Keenan's, vision in his right eye!

On April 11, 2021, my son woke up unable to see out of his right eye. He was told that he had an infection in the eye. After further testing, he was diagnosed with an autoimmune illness that was deemed incurable. I reached out to Pastor Emmanuel, and we prayed. I am happy to say that my son's vision has been completely restored!!! To God be all the glory.

N'Krumah celebrates the preservation of life!

Hello CCCG! I have come to testify of God's awesomeness and to give Him thanks for the preservation of my life. This is just the first of many, by the way. Testimonies galore!!!

So for the past couple of months, I wasn't feeling like myself. I lost a lot of weight and was feeling extremely tired. During the last week of

March, I visited my doctor who ordered some tests to be run. On April 1, the day of Come and See, and the week Pastor told us to pray in the Spirit for an hour each day, my doctor diagnosed my enemy with End Stage Chronic Kidney Failure (Stage 5). He also said that there were some things going on with my enemy's heart. Earlier that week, I was told that there were some concerns with my enemy's lungs as well. My doctor told my wife and me that I would need to be hospitalized the next day as a matter of urgency.

After leaving the doctor's office, I called Pastor Emmanuel to update him. He prayed with my wife and me, and he said, "You will testify!" At the end of our conversation with Pastor, before he got to hang up the phone properly, we could hear Pastor Emmanuel praying in the Spirit.

Fast forward to three hours later… While at home preparing to take a bath, I had a seizure and was found unresponsive in the bathroom. My wife called the ambulance and then Pastor Emmanuel. I don't remember much about that day, but what was evident was that the devil was trying to take me out…but God!!!

Pastor Emmanuel called my wife later that evening to check in and to say, "It is well!" He advised her during that call that the spirit of death had been over me but it is now gone! Pastor went to battle with the devil for my life y'all! He told the devil, "You cannot have him!" While everyone thought Pastor Emmanuel was preparing and resting up for Come and See, he was fighting the devil for the preservation of my life.

You all remember that I live in The Bahamas right? This truly shows that there is no distance in prayer AND the importance and benefits of being under spiritual authority. Today, I am out of hospital after a two-week stay. I am making great progress, by the special grace of God.

Listen, like I said, this is just Part I. This testimony gets better! Like Fritz would say, "stay tuned for Part II." I want to say thank you to my Heavenly Father, my Jehovah Rapha, my Jehovah Shalom, my Jehovah Jireh...You are indeed more than enough! To my spiritual father, Pastor Emmanuel, thank you! Thank you for answering the call of God on your life. I am so blessed to be your son and a part of this great ministry. CCCG family, please continue to keep my family and me in your prayers.

Update from N'Krumah's wife:

I realized that each time my husband had a seizure since being home from the hospital, it happened shortly after he took this particular medication. Being guided by the Holy Spirit, we immediately stopped the medication and decided to monitor his blood pressures closely, documenting the numbers. From that day to this, my husband has not had a seizure and his blood pressures have all been within normal range!

At our follow-up visit with my husband's doctor, which was five days after stopping the medication, his doctor advised us that he was pleased with the numbers and told us to discontinue the medication indefinitely!

We thank God not only for filling us with wisdom in problem-solving and for giving us access to the voice of the Holy Spirit, but we also thank Him for healing my husband from hypertension after 13 years!

To God be ALL the glory!

FINANCIAL BREAKTHROUGH

It amuses me when I hear Christians say that it is not God's will for them to prosper. My question to them is, "If you identify as a child of God, do you know that your Father is the creator of the universe and owns everything in it?" God himself declares in Haggai 2:8 that *"The silver is Mine, the gold is Mine."* How is it that you can settle for a life that is short of the abundance of God when it is very clear that God wants His children to prosper? The Bible says that through prosperity, the word of God will spread across the nations of the earth.

In the group of disciples that followed Jesus, some enjoyed the abundance of God. Joseph of Arimathea was one of them. The wealth God gave him granted him access to the right connections to request Jesus' body. While the other disciples were ardent followers and desired to go to the end with Christ, their lack of abundance restricted how far they could go at that time.

Mary was another one of Jesus' disciples that lived in abundance. She and a few other ladies cared for Christ from their resources. Lydia is also another example. She was wealthy in the land because of the valuable materials she sold and made a profit. In those days, purple linen was a sign of wealth, so anyone who possessed this material was considered prosperous.

When we accept the blessings of God, it positions us to also be a blessing to others through our resources. I believe that the average Christian knows that God wants them to be financially stable, but the issue most Christians have is that they do not think that God wants them to enjoy abundance. Oddly, it is a stigmatized concept in Christendom.

Financial breakthrough can be defined as having enough financial resources to do all God has called you to do and be all He has made you to be. Often, the desire for a financial breakthrough is stirred up when we witness an unfortunate event or situation take place and wish we could do more than be sympathetic. Financial abundance is not the same as selfishness or materialism, it is bigger than our wants. A part of our purpose is to finance God's wants and the needs of His kingdom.

If you desire prosperity so you can have the latest and greatest of worldly possessions, then you have it completely wrong. Note my use of the word *desire*. Matthew 6:33 tells us that our desire must be for the Kingdom of God and its righteousness, not for the latest car, home, or phone, even though God has the capacity to provide those things for us.

Let us take Abraham, for example. We could say Abraham was a billionaire. From the time he left his father's house to the time he died, he amassed an unimaginable amount of wealth that was completely supplied by God. David is another example; he single-handedly supplied up to 70% of the materials needed for his son Solomon to build the temple. I do not know about you, but broke does not look good on anybody. There is nothing holy about it, nor is there anything righteous about it. God even said in Isaiah 45:3 that He will give us the treasures of darkness and hidden riches of secret places to validate that He is God.

We should aspire for abundance, but never to the extent that we become greedy. We must always avoid the pitfall of greed. Many start well but get caught in the web of prosperity. Scriptures make it known that if we chase after money, it will develop wings and fly away. Essentially, you become what's known as a *"paper chaser."* You must be very careful to guard your heart against the love of money because it truly is the root of all evil. If you are not extra careful, you will find that your focus will shift away from God to money. Even though it is God's will for us to prosper, it is never His will for us to begin to worship money. Money must never be your motive for doing anything.

All through your journey of prosperity, ensure that you have a greed-tracker. You are already swimming in dangerous waters when you find it difficult to give to God and those genuinely in need. The goal of greed is to hoard resources, while God's goal of financial abundance is to be a channel of God's resources.

We have evidence that God is still performing financial miracles. As you meditate on the following testimonies from real people, may your faith be strengthened as you trust God for your financial miracle.

Moyo A. celebrates financial abundance in her academics!

I would like to celebrate the God of turnaround! I tried to apply for a bursary in my school multiple times but was always rejected. Another application came out again, and I didn't bother to apply this time. One day I checked my email only to see an email stating I had been successful in getting the bursary. I smiled and knew this was God making me smile...

Secondly, I had been trying to save for education in Canada for several years, but it was never enough. As the years passed, it began to look like I was running out of time. While on my way to work in England, I heard in my spirit that I should give all my savings to sponsor the education of another student struggling with school fees. Though it was all the savings I had for my education, I obeyed and remembered what Pastor said, "If what you have is not enough, what you have is a seed." To the glory of God, today, I am a post-secondary graduate! I did not have to use any of my external savings as God has settled that aspect for me.

Aluisine K. celebrates financial increase!

While learning about financial prosperity at church, I caught a word for financial breakthrough. I waited in expectation for the manifestation of this word. Low and behold, God delivered on His promise on April 30th, the last day of the month. Through the leading of the Holy Spirit, my spiritual father sowed a seed and released verbal blessings into my life. As you may guess, I was over the moon, even more so for the spiritual implications. By the grace of God, this event marked an awesome spiritual transition for my finances and my spiritual growth. This "transition" is loaded, and as things unfold in the coming months by the amazing grace of God, you will hear the unpacked version. I give all the glory to God for His faithfulness and privilege of being a divinely-led Cornerstone family.

Update: As of the publishing of this book, Aluisine has landed profitable financial opportunities and is thriving.

Kadimay S. celebrates financial breakthrough!

I sowed a seed on the last day of the advanced leadership class, and in doing so, I trusted God for financial breakthrough and favour. Not too long after, I got called in for a very good job with an amazing salary. I was favoured because I don't have experience in this job. God made a way for me, and I was favoured in the eyes of my employer, so praise God.

Jayne B. celebrates financial blessings, debt cancellation, and business expansion!

The Lord reminded me of what I prayed for one Sunday. During one of our pre-service prayers, Pastor Emmanuel told us to ask for something we wanted. I prayed and asked God to cancel my debts. I remember I almost felt a sense of condemnation because I didn't ask for anything concerning the church. The enemy was trying to tell me that I was selfish for asking God to cancel my debts. But God is faithful.

The Lord sent an individual in the church to connect me with someone that offered to do my business taxes. Not only did she educate me on how to properly set up systems for my business she also taught me how to properly optimize my business expenses. Moreover, she filed my taxes for FREE! As a result of her expertise, I received a refund instead of owing the government because she educated me on what I was allowed to claim.

As instructed by the Holy Spirit, I used my tax refund to pay off the remaining debt on my vehicle, and that debt has officially been paid off. I prayed for God to cancel my debts on Sunday, and by Tuesday, I paid off my vehicle! The financial abundance I have begun to experience will continue in Jesus' name. The number of new clients I have received this month has almost tripled since last month. Last month I received two new clients, and this month I have received five new clients to the glory of God. Thank you, Lord, for giving me the grace to never give up and increasing my capacity to manage the increase.

Kayode O. celebrates financial abundance to pay off a significant amount of debt!

I want to thank God for everything He has done in my life. I was reminded that I have so many testimonies that I haven't thanked God for yet. Over a short period of time, I have been able to pay off two different debts, amounting to over $11,000. I've also been able to reduce other debts significantly. Looking at my income and how much I have been able to pay off in a short time frame, it's very clear that if not for God, all this wouldn't have been possible.

Landon K. celebrates miraculous financial provision!

Good morning family. For a while now, I have been struggling with opening my mouth in prayer and declaring what I want to see happen in my life. I just let things happen to me.

Recently my family and I have been a little tight on money. I felt compassion for my dad and wanted to help him by praying for him and our family's wealth. So, I declared that we would have enough money for everything we needed to pay for and help each other out. The next day before noon, I got two paycheques from my old job that I had forgotten to pick up that my boss dropped off at my door. Thinking back to the other night, I realize I got exactly what I prayed for. It reminded me to put everything in God's hands, even when we believe we know a way out for ourselves. I'm really grateful to God for this humbling experience because it just reminds me how much He loves me, which helps me to love him more and more.

Aminata M. celebrates miraculous financial provision!

There was a time I needed a significant amount of money to take care of something but did not have enough to do so. One day, I sat down in my room, contemplating how to resolve this need. Suddenly I remembered a personal testimony and lesson my Spiritual Father taught me about having power and dominion over money. Faith quickly rose within me, and I prayed a quick prayer committing the entire matter over to God, asking that he make provision! I then declared, "money come," as taught by my Spiritual Father.

After this, I continued with my life and truthfully forgot about the entire thing. Several weeks later, during one of our programs at church, I received a phone call. I couldn't pick up the call because I was in the service. However, later that evening, as I drove home, the person called back. I answered the call, and the person shared how God laid in their heart to bless me with two things. The first was money, and the second was a vacation. The person then asked me to drop off a particular kind of meal for them at their work and pick up what they had for me. I responded, "You know this is perfect timing because my current location is just one exit away from the restaurant." The person replied, "Interesting because something just pushed me to call you back at this particular time." When I arrived at their workplace to deliver the meal, they handed me a significant amount of money that turned out to be more than what I initially needed!

Look at the God I serve! The God of abundance even added a vacation to the mix. I think He was tired of hearing His princess cry about catching a break from Edmonton. There's no need that God cannot take care of; in fact, He always gives more than what's needed because He is abundant!

Samuel O. celebrates financial provision!

I would like to thank God for His faithfulness in my life. After returning from a trip to Nigeria that cost me a considerable amount of money, I had not worked for a month and two weeks. I needed to work more hours to meet the financial commitments I made for the year. Upon my return, I started working vigorously, I looked forward to my next pay. When my pay came, the Holy Spirit instructed me to give the whole amount to a ministry I am associated with. They needed some audio-visual equipment to make their broadcasting better. I tried negotiating with the Holy Spirit to give part of it, which was still a considerable amount, but the instruction was clear, so I obeyed. After sowing the seed, I kept saying to myself, "If I can just get some free cash right now, it would go a long way in balancing things."

A few days later, Landon shared a testimony of how his former employer sent him a cheque he was not expecting, and I was like, "This is it! God, I key into his testimony! Please give me some free cash that will enable me to balance my finances." So, I started waiting, then later I actually forgot about the whole thing. I got my regular pay as usual on a Friday, and then on Monday morning, while checking my account, I saw an increase in my account balance. I later found out it was from my employer. I was surprised as I was not expecting any money. So, I logged into my company account to look at my pay stub and discovered that I was given a bonus!! By the grace of God, things are now balanced, and we are still on track with regard to the year's commitment. Thank you, Holy Spirit. Hallelujah!

Shaundica E. celebrates an increase in finances!

I'd like to thank God for increase. My husband and I asked God for an increase in our finances. Our prayer was answered. Within days of making a declaration that it would happen within that week, I was promoted on my job, receiving an increase in salary.

Doreen R. celebrates Divine favour and provision for school tuition!

I thank God for His Divine Favour. I had an appointment with our children's school to arrange payment for their school fees for the next school year. In previous years, we would qualify for a discount on their fees; however, based on our combined 2020 income "on paper" to their accounting office, we most likely would not qualify for a discount this next school year.

When it came time to submit our notice of assessments to their office, I had two choices: email them and cancel my appointment or forward our documents and keep the appointment. I trust God, so of course, I kept my appointment!

A day before the appointment, I received a phone call from the school's accounting office. The lady I spoke to informed me that based on our combined income last year, we would not qualify for a reduction in our school fees. This could have easily been the end of the conversation, but she did not stop there. Pay close attention to who your divine helpers are, for this is not the first time she has gone out of her way to favour our family. She continued to ask me about our current financial situation and if the restrictions have impacted our business and personal income this year. Even though "on paper," we should not have qualified for any discount, she wanted to meet with me to discuss how much they could reduce our fees. In the end, she gave us a 40% reduction (almost $1500) from us initially having to pay 100% of tuition for our three children. To God alone be all the glory, Hallelujah!!!

Jayne B. celebrates deliverance from the fear of lack!

I want to thank God for divine provision. Last month my enemy got a flat tire and had to have it replaced. This affected the income that I would have received for the month of May bc I had to cancel some teaching opportunities. This along with some changes in my teaching schedule resulted in only receiving about a quarter of the payment I would usually receive from that particular facility.

Usually, my enemy would get really concerned about this type of situation and try to figure out a solution on my own. But after the teaching on dying to ourselves, the Holy Spirit revealed to me that I had to die in the area of finances. He led me to speak to one of the leaders, and through that conversation, it was confirmed that the answer was to simply die to myself. I knew that the Holy Spirit had already begun this work in me, so from that day I just left it in God's hands and forgot about it.

A couple of days later, God used a family here to bless my family with a financial gift, which was more than I would have received had

I not had the flat tire. Also during this time, we were gifted with 2 additional financial gifts.

The biggest takeaway from this testimony was the revelation of dying to myself and allowing God to be my only hope. In the same way that Jesus was asleep in the boat in the midst of a storm was the same approach the Holy Spirit has been teaching me to take.

God truly is who He says He is. I'm so thankful because I am no longer bound to the fear of lack or not having enough. To God be the glory!

FRUITFULNESS

There are different aspects of fruitfulness that must be clearly understood. Since man's nature is threefold, fruitfulness should be expected in all aspects of man's being. That is, a man should expect to be fruitful spiritually, emotionally, mentally, materially, and of course, physically. Fruitfulness is a validation of life. Fruitfulness is a confirmation that the life of God is in an individual. Stagnation is the opposite of fruitfulness and is evidence that certain laws are being broken or the devil is actively operating in an individual's life.

In Genesis 1, God introduced the idea of creating man with the instruction to be fruitful and multiply. Verse 28, illustrates how God blessed man with an instruction to *"fill the earth and subdue it; have dominion over the fish of the sea, over the birds of the air, and over every living thing that moves on the earth."* This instruction was not just given to man but also extended to other living things. We watch in amazement at how animals procreate, multiply, and dominate their surroundings without the burden of assisted reproduction or any such thing.

Fruitfulness is conceptually similar to success. It is also similar, in meaning, to progress and advancement. It is the will of God for us to be like Him. God is fruitful, and we, His children, are also supposed to be fruitful. When Jesus started His ministry, He had only a handful of disciples. However, in no time, the number of disciples multiplied exponentially until His death. The disciples continued the ministry of Christ, and the number and quality of disciples continued to increase greatly.

The life of a Christian is to be marked by continual growth and advancement. As a child of God, we must expect to be spiritually fruitful by making disciples of all nations, growing in our relationship with God, and manifesting the gifts and fruits of the Holy Spirit. We must also expect to be fruitful in our thoughts, emotional life, character, habits, and all positive spheres of life. There must be proof of growth and fruitfulness whenever and wherever we are seen.

Jesus was angry at the fig tree because it failed to bear fruit (Matthew 21:18-22). The function of the tree was to feed the hungry, so when it did not grow fruit, Jesus cursed the tree. This was again confirmed in Matthew 7:19 when Jesus affirmed that any tree that does not bear fruit would be cut down. Your Father in heaven is committed to your growth and advancement. He is willing and able to make us fruitful. Are you willing to allow Him to make you fruitful?

The Samaritan woman was unfruitful in her calling and purpose until she had an encounter with Jesus by the well (John 4). It is possible to be alive and not have life. You can be involved in activities but not have anything to show for it. You can be working for years but not have evidence to show you are advancing. You could have given your life to Jesus years ago but still not have any evidence of the fruits and gifts of the Holy Spirit as evidence of your salvation.

The author of the book of Hebrews scolded the church for its lack of spiritual growth. When they ought to have been teachers of the word of God, they were still seeking the elementary principles of the kingdom of God (Hebrews 5:12). Elementary principles of the kingdom of God are things like healing, the love of God, and holiness, for example. Is this a reflection of you? Ultimately, unfruitfulness is a state of activity but no productivity. I decree over you in Jesus' name that you will be productive from today!

We understand from scripture that as a man thinks in his heart, so he is (Proverbs 23:7). It is important that your mind is filled with the right expectations as you believe in God for fruitfulness. Here are testimonies that speak to God's ability to trigger physical, emotional, mental, and spiritual fruitfulness in your life.

Alex A. celebrates promotion in the workplace!

I'd like to Thank God for His favour at work; I recently got called back to work and was reminded that I still hadn't thanked Him for the promotion I received back in June of 2020. Work was looking to promote two new supervisors as a new attraction would be opening up at the end of summer last year. At first, I didn't even consider applying because I knew there were others with the same skills as me with greater seniority, and in my mind, it just made sense that the positions would go to them. I remember overhearing that all the current supervisors got together to give their opinions on who they thought should get promoted. Although my name was mentioned as a possibility, I wasn't among the top prospects, which was a bit discouraging but expected. What wasn't expected was the way God intervened in that situation.

The normal procedure is that people apply for the position, and then there is an interview process with the management team. However, due to the new attraction opening soon, management did away with normal procedure and decided to offer the promotion to the two individuals they saw fit to promote.

One morning I got called into the managers' office with the three of them standing there, and the first thing out of my General Manager's mouth was, "Hey would you like to be a supervisor?" I said, "Sure!" I later asked, "Why me when there were others who were qualified and had seniority over me?" They explained that my track record of going above and beyond had not gone unnoticed and that my unique set of people skills set me apart from the others. My skills would be of great value at the new attraction as it would be customer-focused. I walked out of that meeting filled with joy and awe of God's favour over my life. I thought of the supervisors who had their opinions, and my spirit began to sing, "WHO HAS THE FINAL SAY, JEHOVAH HAS THE FINAL SAY," so I give God all the glory.

Nana S. B. celebrates double promotion in the workplace!

Hello church family. We serve a God that is extraordinary in His ways. God has done it again, and I would like to share this turnaround story and give hope to those in their waiting season. A few weeks ago, Pastor Emmanuel spoke a word over the church during Sunday service that we were entering a week of turnaround. Immediately when I heard it, I held onto it. By Thursday, I had already received favour, but I was reminded that we should expect miraculous favour, and the week didn't mean it would end by that Saturday.

A few days later, there was an opportunity for advancement in the organization for a leadership position. I made my request for that position in the evening, and the recommendation sent forth to upper management was an act of favour in itself. I was thinking that I would receive a response within a week, but by the very next morning, I was promoted with another pay increase for that leadership role. I was also told my training would begin the very next day.

This is my third promotion since I started in January, and it didn't end there as the Lord would have it. On my first official day, I was also scheduled to train others for that same role. My heart is full of gratitude for God's overwhelming favour. Just a few years ago, here in Edmonton, I didn't have the funds to even buy food or pay rent that was due the very next day. But God was so faithful He provided the means that same night.

I can smile now and appreciate those years of waiting where God made requests day and night to give to others and Him. I appreciate those tests and challenging seasons because God was using those situations to deliver me from fear of lack and pride, which has now birthed in me the grace to give freely with joy. I am grateful to God for opening my eyes to see this is beyond me, but there is a responsibility in line to advance His kingdom. I am appreciative of the endless love and continual guidance shown to me through my spiritual parents, Pastor Emmanuel and Pastor Ibukun. They have played a significant role in my restoration and transformation journey.

I acknowledge it was only through God's grace that I could still hold on and continue to follow biblical principles irrespective of how things may have appeared. The Lord continues to show me that He always shows up on TIME!!! When we take care of "His needs," He will take care of ours. God is too faithful to fail and is deserving of all honour and praise for all I that am and will become. Amen!

Ebony F. celebrates the end of stagnation!

Hey family, I want to give a testimony about what God has done and still is doing in my life. For you to understand the magnitude of it, let me take you back a bit. I was always one to start a new project, a new business idea, a new ANYTHING. But the thing is, I NEVER completed any or had the spirit of finisher so every single project in my life has stopped short. Some close to the end and others right at the very start, which left my enemy in a place of stagnation and unfruitfulness.

In November 2021, I met with Pastor and he gave me an instruction to complete an assignment that I had previously given up on (nothing new there, right?). Initially I was extremely hyped but a few days in, things began to shift in my schedule that I didn't account for and discouragement began to set in since my formulas kept unexplainable my failing. The enemy started to tell me that finishing was impossible and encouraged me to give up, and on the final day send a message saying: 'Pastor, I honestly tried my best and this is what I have. Can God meet me where I'm at?'.

Two days before the deadline, the revelation of grace being made available REALLY sank in. Instead of panicking, I began to strengthen myself in God and remembered Pastor's testimony about a course He was doing and also remembered the story he gave about the grace made available to him when he was writing his books and was able to do multiple things at once without feeling stressed.

On November 19th 2021, pastor told me to finish TEN formulas by the end of that month; 11 days to be exact. Not only did I complete ELEVEN formulas, but I also finished a day EARLY. Can you imagine the joy I felt? I finally finished something in my life, and with divine speed! I have NEVER finished a single thing in my life. Just known for a string of unfinished projects and ideas. God knew I needed that victory. The weight of being able to help others bring their ideas and projects to fruition but couldn't do it for myself was beginning to take toll on me and I started to feel like a failure and was literally on the brink of giving up. I was always reminded by others of how 'smart' I am but it began to feel like that wasn't profiting me anything. Having the knowledge, potential and experience, yet still experiencing barrenness in my own life.

I'm now realizing the importance of grace and how it makes us to soar without stress. You'll be surprised at what you can do when you invite God in and He takes over. I know it wasn't in my own strength, but I also know now that I can do all things because of He who strengthens me!

Elvin S. celebrates promotion in the workplace and personal business!

This is a testament to the everlasting mercy and boundless provision of Father in heaven. Romans 12:12 says to *"be joyful in hope, patient in affliction, faithful in prayer."*

At the beginning of 2020, though we were both thankful for jobs that satisfied our financial needs, we worked in toxic work environments that exhausted us mentally and emotionally. My wife had been subjected to abusive behaviour from co-workers and patients, such as being called the n-word and being overlooked for promotions. I also felt overworked and under-appreciated.

In the fall, during my wife's daily hour commute to work, she was struck from behind by a motorist in oncoming traffic on a busy area highway. God spared my wife that day and protected her from fatal or catastrophic injuries. However, the accident left her with a separated shoulder and severe whiplash, requiring at least a year of physiotherapy. The first treatment centre aggravated my wife's injury, prolonging her recovery further.

To God be the glory, He heard our faithful prayers and worked miracles as only he can. Despite the pandemic and state of the economy, I've been promoted twice this year. My wife and I have also launched a new business. This year, my wife was randomly approached at work and offered a higher-paying position with another organization, which she holds today. Regarding my wife's physiotherapy, we found a new treatment center much closer to home, ten times better than the previous experience. Furthermore, after meeting my wife, the facility director offered an incredible opportunity to help grow our business.

All honour, glory, and praise belong to our father in heaven. I thank him wholeheartedly for all He has done and continues to do for us. PRAISE GOD!

Jessica celebrates the birth of her baby girl and the provision of a new job!

I want to thank God for the birth of our baby girl. From the pregnancy to the birth, it could only have been God. During my pregnancy, when I was about 5 months along, I remember calling my husband a few minutes before stepping into the shower to come to have a chat with me. We were chatting, and suddenly, I felt lightheaded, and before I knew it, I was in his arms and blanked out. I fainted for a few seconds, enough for him to carry me from the shower to the bed. I woke up to him calling my name. I give God the glory because God took control and revived me. I also had a terrible stomach bug that got me to the emergency room during that period. My daughter is almost seven months now and growing from strength to strength. It could have only been God.

I also want to thank God for the provision of a new job. Praise the Lord; I got a new job while pregnant! I remember thinking about changing jobs during pregnancy, going from known to the unknown, and having so many other thoughts. Thanks to my amazing husband that the Lord used to encourage and speak to me. I decided to apply for the role. I got called for the interview and appeared with my "little baby bump" in July 2019. The interview was quite exhausting. By the time I was done, I was literally out of breath and simply looking forward to leaving the interview. A few days later I got called, and I was told the organization decided to promote someone internal to the position. There was another position with a similar organization he wanted to submit me for. I told him I wasn't interested. During the July 2019 night prayers, I prayed, saying the job was mine, and I was expecting a callback! A few days later, the recruiter called me back to inform me the organization had decided to create two positions for the same role, and they have decided to hire me for the second position.

Christine N. celebrates the Divine provision of a job!

My dad had been looking for a job for the past eight months, and the search was unsuccessful. Every time he thought he would land a job, he wouldn't. He never mentioned it to me, but I know he was feeling discouraged. In those moments, I would always tell him to stay calm and continue the search.

A few months ago, he was contacted by a company back home and went through a series of interviews with them. Despite the fact that the head of the company had already clearly told him he was the one they wanted for the position, he wasn't excited about the opportunity because he didn't want to move back home. He had already planned to politely decline the offer because he thought they'd ask him to move. Nonetheless, he was willing to work with them if they'd allow him to work remotely.

A few days ago, he called me, and he said he didn't know what to do, so I asked him, "Did you ask God?" I asked Him to ask God and not make any decision until he gets an answer from Him. I specifically asked him to do that because I was worried that he'd make a choice out of desperation and end up in the negative emotional state he was in before leaving his last job. He then told me that he planned to ask the company if they'd be open to remote work during his next interview. To his surprise, it's the company that asked him first if he'd be interested in remote work!

Look at God! God had told me back in January that He was going to provide this job, and He specifically told me (and once almost yelled) to be still. There's power in being still and letting God fight for you. It's a wonderful feeling to go through your prayer list and put a tick next to an item. He is too faithful to fail us!

Ufuoma M. celebrates Divine alignment and direction to the right church!

I'd like to thank God for His daughter Tarissa. In August of 2020, Tarissa invited me to come to check out Cornerstone! At the time, although she had no idea, Cornerstone was the place my soul had been longing for.

I'd also like to thank God for Pastor Emmanuel. The very first day I visited Cornerstone in September of 2020, Pastor Emmanuel had not even started his message, and he said a word from God concerning my life. Since I stepped into this church, I have only moved from glory to glory. So I give God the glory, and I pray, as this church has watered me, may He water every member here, in Jesus' most precious name.

Today I'd like to give thanks for spiritual authority and the access it provides to divine favour! On Sunday after church, I met with Pastor Emmanuel for prayers. One of Pastor's prayer points that really resonated with me was for God to release Fatherly blessings and anointing upon my life.

In this past week alone, I've received not one, not two, but THREE amazing opportunities for growth in my social entrepreneurship pursuits. One was a local organization reaching out to me asking if I'd like to be a part of their advocacy campaign. Not only is it right up my alley, but I will be getting paid to do the things I already do. The second was a full-time, paid research assistant job with a huge national organization—and I did not even apply for it. The third was an associate from a global firm reaching out to me and asking me to join their social entrepreneur program. Not only are these all amazing opportunities, but each of them aligns with the path God has called me to. Even if these things don't come to pass, it shows me the magnitude and speed at which God can release his blessings.

Nifemi A. celebrates Divine acceleration in business!

First, I'd like to give God all the glory and adoration for His Divine favour, grace, and protection this past month. June is my birthday month, and it has been nothing but swift acceleration. At the start of May, I had the opportunity to go to Ghana for a photojournalism internship, but the Lord closed that door because it would have been more of a roadblock than a blessing.

At first, I was a bit worried that I wouldn't get a good job this summer, but I fully trusted that God would amaze me. During this time, the Lord gave me clear instructions to revamp my business plan as I waited. Doing that through May, by May ending, through the referral of a friend, I landed a job interview with a well-known fashion designer who has had her works showcased in New York Fashion Week. She didn't ask for my resumé but to meet with me. We spoke, and she hired me that very day. I intended to support her with social media marketing services, but instead, I landed a more prominent role as the Creative Strategist and Project Assistant of her fashion business. This was God's favour as, through it, the Lord continues to pour unto me the vision of larger service-hood spaces that He will place me in Jesus' name.

Secondly, I'd like to thank God for allowing one of my fashion multimedia storytelling to go GLOBAL. I currently have my work displayed in a gallery in Glasgow, United Kingdom. Some of you might recall my question last year, "How can one find the balance between being a creative artist and not of this world?" This question was deep for me because I was being made aware of certain things in my industry. A few weeks after that sermon, I met with Pastor to further expand my understanding, and what he told me was that my industry is the most spiritually driven out of the others. That was why, as I was increasing my relationship with Christ, the more I would experience forces that wanted to block his light. At one point, I was so close to giving up on being a creative artist because I feared that my light would be doomed if I tried to enter the heart of my industry as a pure Christian Creative. But Pastor's counsel always applies hope.

What truly stuck to me that day from what he said was that "When you create, you're creating from your spirit." This led me to be in a period of beholding in the majority of 2020 to dive deeper into the clear vision God wanted me to execute for his glory. Through the Lord's guidance in doing my best to stay diligent, clarity surrounding this year's community projects emerged fruitfully. The work I currently have displayed at the exhibition is called Gyal on Roads: a photo documentary about conscious movements in faith. By the grace of God, the work is being used as a godly point of reference for Christian Creative internationally. And for non-Christian creatives to see that the power of God is REAL.

Thirdly, I'd like to thank God for the series of fashion editorial publication opportunities I've received from global fashion magazines.

Lastly, by the grace of God, I'll be marketing my business at the Black-Owned Market vendor event on July 24th, 2021.

Seun A. celebrates Divine placement in a home church and the birth of a new business!

The first thing I want to thank God for is for providing me with a church family. Even though I got saved a long time ago, since I came to Canada in 2017 I was struggling with my spiritual growth. Before moving to Edmonton, I found Cornerstone online, and I felt God was leading me to the church. This was confirmed when I had a dream a few months ago. I am so grateful for the opportunity to now serve at Cornerstone. I also want to praise God for providing me with a new business, as well as my first car this year! Looking back on last year, things were vastly different from now. I believe 2021 is my year of supernatural favour.

Ibukun A. celebrates financial provision for her business!

I want to thank God for His divine favour concerning my business. I had a chat with my spiritual dad concerning the next steps for my business, which included reaching out to someone in regards to applying for some grants and benefits. As I did and looked more into the options, I had misread one of the grants, which I thought I did not qualify and left it. Later, the person I reached out to reminded me to apply. I stated I didn't qualify for it. As I pondered on the specificity of the instruction from my spiritual authority, I went back to the link and discovered I had misread the eligibility criteria. I applied, and I was approved for the grant.

Olanrewaju O. celebrates the blessing and covering of tithing!

Hello everyone, I want to thank God for being faithful and for His mercy over me. At the end of December, my car got stolen and was recovered within five hours with very minimal damage to my command starter device in the car because they thought it was a tracker. Recovering a stolen car in five hours is hard to hear these days, so I want to thank God for his faithfulness.

Also, when this incident happened, I remember I had some tithes I was owing because I kept procrastinating to pay them. This incident reminded me not to joke about tithing and not take it for granted anymore. This has helped me fight my bad habit of procrastination because I started paying my tithes diligently. Now, to the glory of God, it's really paid off because I have been getting a lot of favours from my clients in my side business. For example, I'll do a haircut, and clients would pay me way more than I expect, and I'll think they made a mistake and contact them to confirm, and they'll say that's all for me.

So I want to thank God once again for being faithful and merciful. And I'd like to advise anyone else who is always procrastinating with their tithes to try God and be diligent with their tithes and see how God will favour and bless them more abundantly. And I also want to thank God for Pastor Emmanuel for explaining and elaborating on the importance of tithing in general to me. Thank you, Lord.

Tarissa W. celebrates Divine instruction and provision in her business!

Good Morning, Church. I want to thank God for his Divine favour, blessings, and grace! He truly has been good. I've been holding off on sharing this testimony because I was waiting for God to be finished—until I realized that God would never be finished. He is only getting started.

There are so many parts to this testimony, but I'll share the major parts. A few days before February night prayers, I was doing my devotions when I heard God say, "Fear not, for I am with thee." I remembered Isaiah 41:10 and went to read the full chapter. God started speaking immensely through this chapter about the business I wanted to start.

February night prayers came, and I heard God tell me it was time to leave my job. I wasn't sure when God wanted me to leave, but all I heard God say was "five." I shared this with Pastor the same night and told him about how God was ministering to me through Isaiah 41:10.

He started smiling (because little did I know that this scripture would be the scripture for the month of March). He continued to say that we should pray about the timeline of when to leave my job. That Sunday after night prayers, the Holy Spirit told Pastor that April 5th would be my last day at my job. This was exactly five weeks from that Sunday.

I knew this was an instruction from God, but anxiety and worry started to kick in. At this time, I was only getting one cake order a week or one cake order every two weeks. I started thinking about how I will pay my bills and tuition. I even started calculating upcoming orders to see how much income would be coming in and started cancelling unnecessary subscriptions.

I finally started to ask God for peace. Peace to trust him and leave it in His hands. I remembered His words, *"Fear not, for I am with thee."* On March 14th, I wrote my resignation letter and intended to give my two weeks notice on Monday, March 16th. On Sunday, March 15th, my manager texted me that because of COVID, all elementary schools were being closed down but instructed me to still come to work on Monday. I felt the Holy Spirit telling me to wait to hand in the letter. I waited, and the following Wednesday, I got a notification that I was being laid off. I started smiling and thanking God because I realized this was what God was preparing me for. He was testing me to see if I was going to be obedient to his instruction.

I saw this as a blessing because I never had the time to perfect my skill between school, work, and extracurriculars. Now God provided me the time, and I was still getting money through the government funding. Because of COVID, I've had to cancel vacations, which has also allowed me to get money back and put a lot of my travel savings towards start-up expenses!

I want to thank God because I've seen my skill level grow so much. I've gone from having one cake order a week to having five to six cake orders a week, and have even had to decline orders. I know this can only be God because I haven't even launched my business yet. This past Mother's Day, I had 13 cake orders, something that, without grace, I could never imagine doing. When you put your trust in God, He will never fail you! I thank God for providing peace, understanding, favour, and grace in a time that COULD have been filled with uncertainty. Praise be to God!

Al Kamara celebrates the end of career stagnation!

Two years and two months of career stagnation terminated.

My last contract ended on June 21st, 2019, and because of my professional experience and the domain I work in, I was so confident I can easily get another contract role. So, I spent much of the following two months with family. Then I started looking in earnest. I would do promising interviews, thereafter I would get a weird dream and that would be the end of it. No job offer would follow. In the meantime, I got family challenges that nothing in my experience had prepared me for, much less able to resolve on my own.

I prayed, fasted, worshipped with my substance, but there was no change in my situation. In the flesh, things even got worse. While I had occasional moments of discouragement, quitting God was never a remote option for me. My resources dried up and at some point, I could not even bring an offering to God. All the while, my spiritual father, Pastor Emmanuel would reassure me that there is a light at the end of the tunnel, even if there was no indication of anything changing. Then I transitioned from focusing on my problems to praying kingdom advancement prayers and for those in similar situations. When COVID restrictions ended, I immersed myself into kingdom service, both in church and on the harvest field. At this time, I was living on credit card for everything, including gassing up to go to church and for evangelization. To the glory of God, my joy remained intact. Some of you may remember the seed my spiritual father sowed in my life recently, as a spiritual prelude to things turning around for me.

When I got the call for the job offer, I had just accepted, I was in the harvest field. And at every step of the interview process, I would ignore my usual urge to prioritize thorough preparation, rather I would always give priority to a kingdom task I may have at hand. And for each of the two interviews, God's favour flowed liberally. Without sweaty declarations, the source of that weird dream was shut down. By God's grace, I am starting my new role on Monday, August 30.

I came back to give all the glory to God, the terminator or career stagnation and the restorer of dignity. By strength alone, no man can prevail.

MARRIAGE

From the time in the garden, it has been in the heart of the Father to couple His children. God would have never created Eve if Adam was at his best as a single man! Everything God does, He does with purpose and intention. Adam was incomplete, so Eve was created to fill a specific area in his life.

So, that settles it! God wants you to be married. Never question if it is His will for you, unless He specifically instructs you to do otherwise. You may argue, what about the eunuchs like Apostle Paul? Eunuchs are exceptions and we do not build doctrines based on an exception God makes! If God were to instruct you to abstain from marriage and live a life completely devoted to Him, your case would fall into the category of an exception. The fact that God made you a eunuch does not mean you should present it as a foundational Christian doctrine that everyone else must follow.

In Ecclesiastes 4, the Bible says that it is not good for a person to be alone because life is much more enjoyable with the right person. You can surround yourself with family and friends, but what happens when they move on to get married? You are left alone. I pray that this will not be your portion, in Jesus' name! In 1 Corinthians 7:1-9, Apostle Paul made it very clear that he desired everyone to abstain from marriage as he did. Without self-control in sexual desires, he knew they would not be able to sustain themselves like he was able to. Hence, any person who lacks self-control with the opposite sex should trust God to be married to avoid temptations of sexual immorality.

Anyone trusting God for marriage must patiently desire it according to God's timing. When you lust after marriage, you desire something that God already wants to give you, but you seek it at the wrong time or in the wrong way. Why be a victim of sexual immorality when you can wait and honour God and your loved ones by doing things the right way?

When God created you, He had someone in mind who would walk alongside you on the journey of life. Your job is to allow God to direct you in locating that person. This process is not one to be done alone. God has provided you with the tools you need to ensure peace and clarity as you wait or search. You can utilize prayer, fasting, and spiritual authority to confirm your choice before making a marriage commitment.

If you are reading this book and are someone that has missed God's perfect will for you in marriage (and are concerned about it), I have good news for you. God can restore what you have lost. He is able to make all things work together for your good. Yes, you may suffer a little, but believe God will turn things around in your favour. With God, hope is never lost. Never bring God down to your level of reasoning; believe that God can do everything that He says. Abigail's unfortunate marriage to a man like Nabal is a good example. Imagine who might have been married to Jabez before he believed God to turn his life around. There are many ways God can turn your marriage around for the better if you can only believe Him without taking matters into your own hands.

If you have desires for the opposite sex and you are not yet married, regardless of your age, you can confidently ask God to lead you to the right spouse at the appropriate time. Let me repeat, regardless of the mistakes you have made in the past, if you are born again, old things have passed away, and all things have become new (2 Corinthians 5:17). The consequences of your actions may still remain, but I can assure you that God has the best in store for you. This promise also applies to sex workers. Once you have repented, rely on the mercy of God that is everlasting and refreshed on a daily basis.

Doreen R. celebrates the supernatural restoration of her marriage!

In my 20s, I fell in love and got married two years later. I put my husband on a pedestal. Suddenly two months later, he told me that he married a woman he didn't love, left the relationship and travelled back to his country of origin. I was devastated. I hid everything and was ashamed to tell my family about everything, so I protected him and kept it to myself. I started surrounding myself with people that wouldn't help the situation. Fast forward to a couple of years later, we reconnected. Though it was a long-distance relationship, we decided we'd try to make things work. Unfortunately, things didn't work out as I hoped, as we were now having challenges with infidelity, and trust was once again broken. At the time, I knew God, but I didn't have a relationship with Him. I didn't have healthy support systems to support me either.

We continued to work on the relationship for the next couple of years. Things were up and down, but we hit a milestone; we were expecting our first child! We continued to work on things, and then our twins came, but even during this time, there was still infidelity. I was heartbroken and confused; I didn't know what to expect. I had enough but didn't know where to turn. I pushed away my family and friends in an attempt to protect "my family." I cried many nights and looked at myself in the mirror, wondering, "Who are you?" In the midst of all of this, I lost my dad, the one man I compared my husband to. I was broken, but I continued to push through tears and suicidal thoughts.

Fast forward to my 40s, and the transformation that has taken place has changed my life! To the Glory of God, God came through and opened up two doors to me—one of which was the journey of fitness, taking care of myself, and the other was my spiritual journey. Fitness took care of the physical, but I needed help with the mental and spiritual aspects of things; it was also during this time that my husband started attending CCCG leadership classes. I saw a change in my husband, which gave me hope! He eventually started attending CCCG with the children while I stayed at home. Eventually, I joined my family and found myself and my marriage coming out of a dark place. The presence of God in Cornerstone ministered to me every time; the more I attended, the more I learned, and the more the Holy Spirit was helping me. I praise God because my marriage is now restored. I am the happiest I've been, and I look forward to where God is taking us.

Update: As of the publishing of this book, Doreen and her husband celebrated 18 years of marriage, a total of 20 years together!

Towo A. celebrates the supernatural restoration of his marriage!

Hallelujah, August 2020, makes our marriage four years. I bless God for what He has done so far. It has not been easy. It's been tough, but God has been in the storm with us. When we got married, during the wedding a lot of things happened. Prior to getting married, we made sure we sought the face of God and ensured it was His will for us to get married. During the wedding, there were hiccups and issues involving family members. Unknown to us, seeds were being sowed. My wife and I decided we would not go down that route. Those who had issues had to figure them out on their own.

We soon left Nigeria and relocated to the United Kingdom. Other challenges soon came up that were targeted at my wife. We prayed and brushed it aside, not knowing the enemy was also sowing seeds. Within a two-year time frame, more issues resurfaced. It affected our communication and we struggled to understand each other. There were times when I would say something, and my wife would hear a completely different thing, which eventually became quite serious. At this time, so many people had different things to say. We heard many things from different places, and the advice was often very unhelpful. Some even encouraged us to separate, as it was not too late. God held us together though.

We then moved to Canada, and by this time, there was a huge strain on our marriage. At face value, you would not be able to tell, but the state of our relationship was bad. I recall an occasion when we were coming for the basic leadership class. At that time, we had a disagreement, and my wife was packed and ready to leave. We came to a point where I would settle with whatever happened.

During the class, I remembered a dream I had. In this dream, I saw myself trying to tame a wild bull. I would tame it down, and then it would get loose. As this cycle continued, I saw Pastor Emmanuel and Pastor Ibukun standing to the side, watching me. I later got the understanding from the scripture Mark 3:27 *"who can go into a strong man's house and take up his possession without first binding him'*. So, I got an understanding that I wasn't able to bind this stronghold, and it was related to strongholds and curses that we were not capable of holding down. After the class, I explained everything to Pastor Emmanuel and Pastor Ibukun. They prayed for us and declared an end to any curse. They explained that it was that day that we truly began our marriage. Ever since then, things have been so good to the glory of God!

DOMINION OVER FORCES OF DARKNESS

The subject of dominion over demonic forces is one that every Christian should explore and understand to maximize their purpose on the earth. The devil is not omnipotent, omniscient, or omnipresent. This means that he does not have all the power on the earth, does not know everything, and can only be in one place at a time. The devil only has the power to deceive, manipulate, and tempt.

The Bible tells us that we have been given dominion over principalities and powers of darkness, and nothing shall harm us. In fact, in Ephesians 1 and 2, we are told that we are seated in heavenly places far above principalities, powers, and rulers of darkness. When you become aware of the authority you have access to, no devil can successfully defeat you! Jesus demonstrated authority over the devil and his forces in His ministry on the earth. In fact, Acts 10:38 tells us of how God anointed Jesus to deal with demonic forces and actions. Jesus, in turn, handed over that same power to us in Luke 10:19, where He said that we have been given authority to deal with the devil and, as a result, we should not be hurt by the devil.

To understand this transfer of authority, you need to comprehend verse 18 of Luke 10, where Jesus describes watching satan fall like lightning from heaven. Just at the sight of satan falling, Jesus knew that satan would forever be under His feet and that He would always have dominion over him. You and I need to grasp this same revelation to exercise dominion over the devil. In Galatians 4:1, we are told that an heir that is only a child is no different from a slave, and verse 2 goes further to say that the same heir will remain under guardians and stewards until an appointed time. From verse 3, we know that only children remain in bondage, under the elements of this world, and those elements are under the control of satan. This means satan still has leverage over born-again Christians who refuse to grow spiritually. No matter where you find yourself now, understand that it is never God's will for the devil to molest, harass, or successfully attack you.

Every child of God can be empowered to resist the devil and get him to flee from you. In some of my messages on spiritual warfare available on our Cornerstone Christian Church of God Youtube channel, I taught about the authority we have as believers and how to exercise that authority to achieve what Jesus Christ said we could achieve. Remember, Jesus stated that if we believe in Him, we will also be able to do the works He did in greater dimensions (John 14:12). Hence, if Jesus casted out demons, we can cast out demons. If the Apostles casted out demons, we can cast out demons. If Jesus dominated the devil, we can dominate the devil. If the Apostle Paul dominated the devil, we can also dominate the devil.

In 2018, while I was in my Edmonton office, I suddenly began to feel feverish, and it degenerated very quickly. After rebuking several times, I rose from my desk and began to inquire from the Holy Spirit to understand how I was feeling. I heard the Holy Spirit say that what I was feeling was due to an attack the enemy launched against ministers of God in the land. The Holy Spirit then instructed me to call my wife and ask her to anoint herself with oil on behalf of the both of us. The summary is that this battle ended, and I was still standing.

Many other believers worldwide are also walking in dominion over the devil in diverse ways. I declare that from today, you are one of those who will stand and take dominion over the devil in every area of your life!

Kaiha M. celebrates deliverance from fear!

I want to thank God for delivering me from the spirit of fear. Because of the way I grew up and some experiences I had as a young girl, I learned to subdue myself to fear as a form of shielding myself from hurt or opposition. I didn't realize how much pain I was carrying until I heard pastor speak about the demonic systems of control. I realized I had shifted my whole life to accommodate the pain in my life because it felt like my only chance at relief. Little did I know, that meant I was surrendering to the hold of fear. Things that I should have been doing with boldness became difficult for me because fear would paralyze me and I would just remain inactive. It would cause me to overanalyze, to shrink myself for others, and to never feel like enough, even when I have seen God work through me. But today I'm grateful because His grace is enough and it has pulled me out. I thank God because I have understanding now, and I am able to walk in boldness. I thank God for using Pastor Emmanuel to speak into my life and help bring me that understanding and deliverance. And I know that it will only continue to grow from here.

Bolakunmi B. celebrates deliverance from spiritual attacks!

I want to thank God for breakthrough, for strength and Grace to stand. About a couple weeks ago, I was attacked spiritually. I felt a strong force trying to hold me down and I began screaming to the force "I belong to Jesus" Moments later I woke up from my sleep and slept back and had the same exact dream with the same outcome. As my spiritual father says you are the first Prophet over your own life, I woke up again and prophesied, said a word over my life and I've never experienced the dream.

Name withheld celebrates deliverance from demonic oppression!

I want to give God all the glory for delivering me demonic oppression.

On Sunday April 18th during the service when Pastor asked if there is anyone who is not saved he would like to pray with them, I was shy to raise up my hands but I said the prayers with him. After the prayer he then said he saw dark birds flying away that was indeed about me. For the past few months I was being tormented by dark birds that would follow me everywhere I went and sometimes people would also notice them. It was really embarrassing for me. After that prayer that Sunday, I no longer see them and I know I'm free and saved forever. Thank you, Jesus

Alex A. celebrates deliverance from the spirit of fear and stagnation!

I want to Thank God for Deliverance from the Spirit of Fear, and Stagnation. The enemy had worn me down so much with his suggestions of me being a failure in various areas of my life over the years that at some point I took ownership of them. When I would try to fight to the suggestions of the enemy he would point to all the failures I've accumulated over the years and it would cripple me because the memories of those lived experiences would play on repeat in my mind. It was a challenge to see myself the way God sees me because His Words over me didn't match my circumstances. With this double-mindedness came stagnation which would just perpetuate a demonic and seemingly endless cycle. My Restoration Process began with a meeting with my Spiritual Father toward the end of September, in that meeting he shared with me what the Holy Spirit had revealed to him. That all things being equal if I didn't leave it all on the altar for God, the image revealed to Pastor was my image but 4 YEARS in Future still in the same position. I had never been as frustrated in my life as I was at that moment. On the drive home I decided that enough was enough, the enemy had made me it's plaything for far too long. I recommitted myself to Christ and despite what may come my way I will fight the Good Fight of Faith and IF I PERISH, I PERISH.

Sionna B. celebrates deliverance from demonic oppression!

I give God all the glory for restoration and transformation here at CCCG, as I was reading the book of the month " Dream like a Child Execute like a pro" by Pastor Emmanuel, I read a part that talked about how fear can be a hindrance in our vision, and Pastor began to share an example about having a sound mind means to not be afraid of the dark, right away The Holy Spirit reminded me how I was so afraid of the dark, I used to date a fella that will encourage me to always sleep with the light on, this increased the fear of the dark to the point where every night I will sleep with my night lamp on(my siblings will laugh at me that I was afraid of the dark) I soon forced myself out of that habit but I will always cover my head while sleeping.(at first I just thought it was my comfortable position to sleep, but the more I thought about it, i knew it was the fear of the dark.)It was so bad that I couldn't even face the door or stare in the dark without feeling like something was there.This fear started because I will get a lot of nightmares & spiritual attack growing up & one included seeing demon when I was only 7 at the time. I would also have panic attacks at night to the point where I felt I had no control of my body because during those attacks I would find myself running to the light to turn it on and not remember how I got out of bed. It was very very bad. But I want to thank God for setting me free ever since I joined this ministry, because now I love dark rooms and I need the dark to meditate and pray all the time, I can stare blank in the dark and talk to Jesus as if He is right there and just feel complete peace of mind, I bless God and give Him all the glory for reminding me of what He did for me.

Gracia M. celebrates deliverance from the spirit of rejection!

Good morning church!

I want to first start off by thanking God for allowing me to be a part of this new family. Before making CCCG my home church, my sister & I felt like we've "outgrown" the church our family was attending. It wasn't until September of last year that our friend Sandrine, invited us to bible study & from there on I never looked back. Though I thanked God for finding us this church, it was still a time in my life I was dealing with a lot of shame & disappointment from past experiences. I'd constantly ask myself & ask God why me? Why is it that others around me are succeeding & I'm not? Are these results of past mistakes? I knew these thoughts weren't from God & so I asked the Holy Spirit for intentional guidance.

Throughout Pastors' teachings & hearing many powerful testimonies, I've realized that I was feeding too much attention to what the enemy was saying. I now declare to myself every morning that I am who God says I am & that I have dominion over my life no matter my circumstances.

Though I'm not perfect & I'm still a work in progress, I can't thank God enough for what He's been doing & still doing in my life. I thank you Pastors for being spiritual authorities in my life.

I want to also quickly thank God for promotion. I thank God for peace of mind & for delivering me from the spirit of rejection! Praise God!

Angela W. celebrates dominion over darkness!

Hello church family! I want to thank God today for the protection he has given me, and giving me the power of association with Pastor. The other day (Sunday night) I went to bed with an uneasy feeling of being tired, and just drained. I prayed to have energy restored and to have an open heart in receiving it as the next evening I was meeting with Pastor. I proceeded to go to bed when I heard my name whispered just as I was about to fall asleep. It was a deep whisper almost trying to invite me into the darkness. I woke up, lights on in every room of the house and prayed for God's protection as there was an uneasy energy or being in my house. I went to bed about an hour later, where I was scared out of my sleep with a nightmare of someone in my room. Again, prayer, lights on pacing back and forth. This went on ALL NIGHT! Let me tell you sis was tired the next day! My meeting with Pastor was just what I needed as Monday night, with a soft heart, eased mind and calm sense of protection I was in bed with no darkness, no uneasy feeling and slept through the night. The Sunday night was the enemy trying to attack as they knew I was meeting with Pastor and talking about the growth of my future and growth in the church. There is power in prayer, power in the association and relationships built in the church and trusting God has me always. Thank you church.

Comfort S. celebrates deliverance from sexual immorality!

I wrestled with sharing this testimony because of the shame and humiliation I felt but the Lord told me to. After testifying about celebrating one year of being delivered and set free from masturbation and pornography, I fell a couple weeks after. When this happened, I couldn't believe it, I was devastated and depressed! I reached out to pastor and he prayed for me. I also prayed and received a couple revelations on why I fell! The Holy Spirit made me realize that I was under attack and that no matter how confident I was, the devil will still try 1 year later, 5 years later and even 10 years later but in those days of battle, we have to choose to flee like Joseph and not fall like David. As much as I hate that I'm sharing this but I know that I'm not the only one that has fallen and I'm here to testify that the Lord has picked me back up and He will pick you back up too!

Doyin O. celebrates deliverance from shame, pain and rejection!

I had struggled with my identity this month, I was praying and fasting and I couldn't even identify my office. The more I prayed and looked inwards, the more I realized that I had been hiding most of my life and didn't know what my true personality was. I met with pastor Emmanuel and during my meeting, pastor mentioned there was a traumatic event in my life that had affected who I was. During the meeting the holy spirit brought to my remembrance shame, pain and rejection I went through as a young girl aged 10 to 12 years old where I was publicly embarrassed on several occasions in my school hostel for bedwetting. These events were buried deep in my psyche and had affected who I was over the years. I had labelled myself as nervous, anxious and would do anything to avoid a situation where I could be embarrassed.

Sandrine A. celebrates deliverance from a destructive lifestyle!

Good morning family.

I had hoped to share this testimony with you last night, but I didn't get the opportunity. I haven't had a good January. Every small mistake I make, the devil will try to use it against me, I've been talking down on myself so much lately, like My enemy can not let breath.(shame on him because here I am). My enemy was attempting to convince me to stand back from the worship team for some time, and he was using the spirit of fear against me to prevent me from singing during worship. He would say things like, "What if you screwed up," "you're not good enough,"

"You should just sit down now before you embarrass yourself," and other things like that, and these comments would hit me like a tonne of bricks. Last Sunday, at the second service, someone shared their testimony about how they were living a destructive life. I was moved to tears as soon as I heard this testimony, and I couldn't stop crying. I didn't understand why at first, and I was perplexed, so I simply lifted it to God. Let's skip ahead to the night prayer. As I prayed, the holy spirit began to remind me of my previous life, encouraging me to be proud of myself and that it's normal to make mistakes. And he told me to take a moment to reflect on where I've come from and appreciate where I am now. He later reminded me that the reason I was overcome with emotion the previous Sunday, Is because I used to live a destructive lifestyle as well. but look at me now. God is wonderful.

1. Sexually assaulted- healed from that trauma.
2. Delivered from the spirit of darkness.
3. Free from the spirit of fear.
4. 3 months sober from alcohol and drugs.
5. Delivered from the spirit of anger.
6. Delivered from the spirit of perfection
7. Protected me in a dark alley- where I was drunk out of my mind with no way of getting home. That alone has its own testimony.

The list goes on and on. I'd like to take this opportunity to thank God for his goodness and mercy throughout my life. I wouldn't be where I am today if it weren't for God, and I'm grateful that he was able to show me and remind me that I am still worthy of his love.

Mekelle celebrates deliverance from fear and rationalization!

I was able to see what spirits were being activated in my life (as well as my loved one's) as a matter of fact the example used at Bible Study for fear was me. It started with fear that coupled with rationalization. My grandpa was knocked down crossing the street many years ago I would like to say back in 1999 and I was just a kid then but when I had to cross the street I would literally wait until there were absolutely no cars coming. It didn't matter to me how long that took. I would at times wait for others to walk across the street with me(it didn't matter who- strangers or friends). I made excuses and even made jokes to minimize the seriousness of it but with revelation I can and will be able to cross the street at ease from now on in Jesus name. Additionally, the combo fear & rationalization hindered me from making certain commitments as well. I thank God for His love and revelation to fulfill the many things He has in store for me!

Allegra M. celebrates deliverance from sexual immorality and addiction!

If someone had asked me how my 2021 was, the old version of me would say it was the hardest year of my life but who I am now, I can confidently say it was definitely a life changing year because of God's mercy.

So let me go a bit deeper. I came into 2021 living a sinful lifestyle. I didn't realize it at the time but I was broken & just very empty inside. Beginning of that year, my sister & I didn't have a home church & my personal relationship with God was very surface level.

I was dealing with sexual immorality and marijuana addiction. Because of that influence, it resulted in me getting pregnant in late April.

When I found out, I was full of fear and shame so I went ahead and got an abortion. After that happened, I went on about my life thinking it wouldn't get to me at all but I kept doing the same things expecting different results ... insanity. So in June I found out I was pregnant again. and that's when I got another abortion. After that, that's when everything went downhill for me. I fell into depression, cried myself to sleep & I would ask God why'd He wake me up in the morning cause I didn't think I was worthy of anything good at this point. I started smoking my pain away cause I felt like there was no way out of this torment.

In August, I got invited to CCCG for a bible study service. At first I was hesitant to go because of past experiences but something kept telling me to go (now I know it was the Holy Spirit) so I went. I remember as soon as I entered the building I just felt God's presence and His love filling me up. I had a little bit of hope that God was able to turn it around so I kept showing up and showing up little by little. Couple weeks after I was able to meet with Pastor E and a lot was revealed & he gave me instructions. God definitely gave me the grace to follow those instructions cause Lord knows!

I've been smoking weed since I was 16 & now I'm 23 and by God's grace I've been delivered from that bondage & I've been celibate for a few months now as well. God found me in a place where I didn't think it was possible to get out of but through His grace, unfailing mercy & His unending love, He transformed and restored my life forever. He gave me the peace & joy I've longed for, so I thank God every single day of my life & I give Him all the praise & all the glory! To Pastor Emmanuel & Pastor Ibukun from the bottom of my heart thank you for welcoming me to CCCG with open arms!

Ifeoma O. celebrates deliverance from career shame!

I want to thank God for delivering me from career shame at the Come and See in November. I was of the mindset that I had no shame. But as the word started coming forth, I was reminded of the career shame that had held me bound over the years and stopped me from advancing in my career. The holy spirit reminded me of two job interviews I had in 2013. At one interview, it ended within 5 mins of starting. At another interview, some people on the panel chuckled/laughed at my response to a question. This question didn't elicit such a response as it was a serious question. I didn't know it affected me over the years. I dreaded interviews and became anxious, incoherent, unable to articulate my skills. I would even pray to get a job without an interview or even look for an excuse to cancel job interviews. At the Come and See conference, I felt a cool air around me with the holy spirit saying, it's okay, I am taking the shame away. Then I keyed into the words Pastor said that God would give double honour for everything we lost due to shame. Since then, I have had interviews, and the holy spirit aided with my preparation by giving me questions to ask. I have been very confident that I felt it might be arrogance. Still, my lovely husband reminded me that interviews are two-way communication, and it's normal to interview the company as well. It can only be God.

ACADEMIC SUCCESS

Faith for academic success starts with coming into agreement with God's will concerning your career path. We sometimes assume that God is not concerned with what we study in school when, in fact, He is very concerned. So much so, that He designed a specific path for you to follow. However, it is up to you to seek His will for you in this area.

Academic excellence is a result of saying yes to God. Allow Him to lead you in whatever direction He plans. When you are in the perfect will of God for your academics, grace is made available to you to ensure you succeed. God's grace secures your success in school, not hours of studying or excessive note-taking. Even though these can be good practices, they do not guarantee success. In the odd case that you get good grades due to relying on your flesh, a lot of sleep would have been lost, together with stress and other unhealthy patterns. The beautiful thing about the grace that God gives is that it is the opposite of everything described in the previous sentence.

Grace for academic success is a supply of energy, an outpouring of wisdom and an infilling of every tool you will need on your academic journey! Tapping into this grace requires you to continue believing God's calling upon your life for where He is taking you. It requires that you make up your mind to confidently believe that God will never call you to a program of study He cannot equip you to do.

2 Corinthians 12:9 enlightens us to how grace works. To sum it up, grace is perfected in us when we are weak. Yes, this means that you must come to the end of yourself for grace to take effect. For God to display wisdom, understanding, strength, and excellence in you, He needs you to stop trying to do everything by yourself. When we step aside and allow Him to do what He has called us to, then we will attain consistent academic success. It is God's will that you are the head of your class, with the best grade on every assignment. Sadly though, as Christians, the mistake we make is that we accept the direction God is calling us in, but rely on our own strength to complete the work.

Think about this: if God knew that you could do His will without His grace, do you think He would call you to do it? The answer is no, because it is contradictory to how He operates. God's will is always set up so that we have no choice but to rely on His grace for it to manifest and continuously thrive. You need God to get that degree with distinction, the same way you need God to pass that exam for the next level of your career. Without the one that called you to it, you will struggle unnecessarily.

I cannot tell you how many times I have painfully watched people struggle with academics because they failed to connect to grace. This is not God's plan for you, and I know that will not be your reality in Jesus' name. Make up your mind now that you will not pursue academic success in your strength. Now, repeat after me, "I am designed for academic success, and I will enjoy academic success in Jesus' name."

God is not asking you to believe He can do something He has never done before. God empowered Daniel to enjoy academic success, and he was found ten times better than his other colleagues. (Daniel 1:20) You will achieve greater academic success than Daniel in Jesus' name. Here are some testimonies that will strengthen your faith in God and His ability to engrace you towards academic success.

Aminata M. celebrates academic excellence!

I want to give God all the glory for academic success! By the grace of God, I just finished the first term of my program, and I finished with A's! God has been so faithful! From giving me the grace to accept His desire for me to be in this field, to getting me into school and fulfilling His promise that I would succeed and that it would be easy to do so! I've just been thinking about how everything has played out over the last couple of days, and I'm grateful to Him, especially for blessing me with my support system. Despite all the interesting things the enemy has been trying, God ensured that His promise concerning my education is fulfilled and will continue to be fulfilled. Where I am now is not what I initially wanted for myself, but I thank God for parents that are committed to seeing you thrive in God's perfect will.

I want to encourage anyone still trying to figure out school, purpose, or the connection between the two. It's important that you know that God has a unique plan for you. Take time to pray and ask Him what these plans are and how your education is tied to them. But ultimately, you have to decide if it's God's will you'll pursue or your own. For me, it came down to doing God's perfect will for my education, even though it was not what I desired at the time but come first place. Or do I do my own thing and take second place in my life? The latter did not make sense because how can I consciously take second place in my life and call it a "fulfilled life?" I chose the first option; that's why I'm here today, enjoying God's grace and favour in school! So, yeah, be encouraged! Quit playing and GO BACK TO SCHOOL (if that's what God is saying you should do). Amen! Praise the good Lord!

Nana S.B. celebrates favour in her academics!

I want to thank God for multiplied grace and continued favour in my academics. I finished strong with a final grade of an A last semester. Initially, I had underestimated the time and dedication required for a postgraduate degree coupled with working full time. I thank God for the authorities over my life (my mother and Pastors) with their words of encouragement and redirection in executing my studies with limited to no stress.

Mercy J. celebrates the supply of grace for academic success!

I also want to thank God for taking me through my school year. At the end of last semester, I testified that my lowest grade out of 6 courses was an A-. Going into that semester, I didn't think very highly of my academic ability, but God turned things around for me. Out of the 6 courses I took this term, my lowest grade was an A, and I'm grateful to God to the point of tears. I give Him all the glory for taking care of me so perfectly. Praise The Lord!

Anna A. celebrates favour and excellence in her academics!

I also want to thank God for His favour in my academics. I worked on the wrong assignment and submitted it. My professor marked it and left feedback saying, "Nice effort but wrong assignment." To my surprise, I was graded a B+. I spoke to my professor and asked if it would be possible to submit the correct assignment; he said it wasn't necessary because he liked everything I wrote on the assignment I initially submitted. The assignment I submitted had nothing to do with what he had been teaching, so he graded me a B+. The mark could have been worse, but I want to thank God for the favour he gave me on the wrong assignment. Amen and Amen!

Marie E. celebrates Divine favour in her academics!

I would like to thank God for a successful school semester. Some of you may remember my testimony earlier this year when God favoured me by dismissing a failing grade for one of my classes. After that testimony, I continued to struggle with this class. Despite the weight of the mid-term exam I failed being transferred to the final exam, I was still very worried that I would not be able to eventually pass the class. Not to mention that I also got COVID in the midst of preparing for my finals, so it seemed impossible.

Not only did God allow me to pass the class, but He gave me a B+. On top of that, He gave me my best academic semester in my undergrad with 3 A's, a B and a B +. This is truly a testimony because I hadn't taken five courses in a semester since my first year, and I never thought I would be able to do that well under such a big workload. Although I had doubts about myself, God knew where He was taking me and the plans He had for me. He refused to allow me to fail. He remained faithful, and I have to give Him praise. Hallelujah!

Mariam S. celebrates overcoming doubt and good grades in school!

I went into school with many doubts, but I knew I wanted to be in school and that the field I chose was what I wanted to do. Throughout the semester, I thank God for giving me wisdom and helping me finish my assignments. Towards the end of the semester, things got hectic at work, which required me to pick up extra shifts. That got in between my studies, but God also saw me through, and I was able to finish my classes with mostly A's. I guess what I want to end with is that even though things in life get stressful, trust in God because He is faithful to see you through whatever you are going through.

Ifeoma O. celebrates supernatural speed and excellence in her academics!

I thank God for school. This semester has been great. I am experiencing supernatural speed with getting my school work done. Also, in the courses I am taking, I don't feel like I am grasping it the way I want to, but God has been helping me pass. He tells me what to write and how to answer questions. It's interesting that my professors comment on my work as excellent and say I understand the coursework even if I feel otherwise. It's all God!

Prisca P. celebrates clarity and direction in the area of her academics!

My major prayer points since the beginning of this year are school and finance-related. I had to make a choice of specialization for the last year of my Master's degree. I wanted to do Marketing, but apart from the fact that I have professional experience in that area, I wanted to do that specific program because it was an apprenticeship; and I wouldn't have to pay any fees. Even though I was convinced I was doing it only because I liked it, deep down there was always so much confusion and discomfort when I'd think about it. The outcomes of that degree were too blurry. I didn't have the money required for tuition, so to me, that was the better option.

The night before applications for specializations would open, I wasn't at peace. My mom had asked me to tell her when they'd open so we could go through the choices together. I accepted reluctantly, but in my mind, I was ready to go to war because I already knew she wanted me to do Finance, and this time, I wasn't going to please her just because! II had already planned to apply and inform her later.

I took a nap, and when I woke up, the Holy Spirit told me, "You want to do the apprenticeship because you are scared of not having the money to pay for your school fees. That number scares you. Open your laptop and choose what your heart actually wants." It was very true. I didn't have those thousands of dollars to pay. So I opened my laptop, and I went on the Business Consulting and Digital Transformation page, and for the first time in a while, I felt an unexplainable peace. It felt like God saying, "Yes child, this is it." I smiled and said, "Okay, then this means that You'll cover my tuition, so I'm waiting for You." Then he said, "Call your parents and talk." My dad said, "With everything you're telling me, I'd encourage you to apply to the business consulting one'" Then my mom said, "Apply for business consulting, but please put financial management as a second choice." When I called Pastor E, he confirmed as well.

So I applied for that degree, and put financial management as my second choice to please Mom, but I already knew that wasn't happening. I applied, and on Monday, I received an email confirming that my application had been accepted!! It's crazy because when I first got to this school, that was the specialization I had in my heart. I thank God for putting me back on the right track!

Kenchera I. celebrates the wisdom and grace to successfully complete her Ph.D.!

Through this movement, I have learned the significance of coming back to say thank you. I am grateful that God gave me the wisdom, knowledge, and understanding to complete my Ph.D. with speed and favour. My final exam should have taken 3 to 4 hours, but within 2 hours, I was complete, and a final decision was made on the success of my defense. I want to thank God for already using this work to minister to the hearts of others about the systematic barriers Black people face inside and outside of the classroom in Canada. I ask God that I will always be mindful to stay humble and give Him the glory. I would also like to thank God that three degrees later, totalling $150,000 plus, God provided through consistent scholarships, and I have zero debt. I thank God because He gave me wisdom and revelation throughout. He directed me on when to apply, how to apply, and where to connect myself for favour and advancement in funding.

Avoid The Extreme

We must avoid extremes if we want our faith to produce results. Some people delay taking action in certain situations because they are waiting to hear God speak to them about the particular situation 'clearly'. If God has already made His intentions about a particular situation known in the Bible, we should not expect that He will repeat it to us again. This is why a child of God should make reading and hearing the anointed word of God a priority in their life. You can never fulfill the objective of your faith without you taking action. Some people mistakenly determine that because God's will for their life is the best course of action, they must do nothing until He audibly tells them to move. They want God to speak to them spectacularly through a dream, angelic visitation, or vision before they take any and every step. Don't overlook the supernatural because you are waiting for the spectacular. The word of God in the Bible is supernatural and gives us answers to many of life's problems. Don't neglect it.

In Luke 22:42, when Jesus prayed for the cup to pass over Him, did you notice that God the Father never answered Him? This is because God knew that Jesus was very well aware of His will concerning that situation. In a case where you are genuinely unaware of the will of God, you can expect Him to reveal it to you directly or indirectly, either through His word or the Holy Spirit. Once you know the will of God, the next step is for you to rise and shine by following it.

Another extreme is to take what God said to someone else and directly apply it to your life without getting that instruction validated by God. Here is an example to help clarify what I am referencing: imagine that an individual testified that God asked them to give away their old car, and someone came and blessed them with a brand new vehicle. It is incorrect to hear that testimony and then give away your old vehicle, expecting someone to give you a brand new car in return.

I can imagine that quite a number of believers have short-circuited their faith and are offended by God because of this gross misunderstanding of how God works. They in turn, become disillusioned because they did what someone else did, but did not get the same results. God is never committed to performing what He did not promise us. You must understand that God's instructions are personalized. Can you imagine a person reading about Abraham's intended sacrifice of his son Isaac and then deciding to follow in the same footsteps? I know you can understand how disastrous this would be.

The bible is a container for God's many instructions given to human beings. How then do we know which of the myriads of instructions apply to each aspect of our lives? The answer is through the leading of the Holy Spirit. God's word promises us divine guidance, so we should not be concerned about the possibility of missing God's plan and His will for our lives. When we hear other people's testimonies, rejoice with them without feeling the need to replicate their testimony in your strength. Our job is to consistently and sincerely rejoice with those who rejoice (Romans 12:15). Let the Holy Spirit be the umpire in helping you decide which of the instructions He gave others that He is also now giving to you.

There is another extreme I want to address; which is believing that you can do anything you want to because you have faith. This extreme is perhaps rooted in the misconception of what Philippians 4:13 actually means. Paul the Apostle made that interesting utterance when he said he could do all things through Christ who strengthens him. Some have taken this scripture to mean that they can do anything as long as they have faith, including what God has not expressly sent them to do. This idea implies that man is omnipotent and is, therefore, incorrect. Only God is omnipotent. What Paul the Apostle was alluding to in that passage of scripture was that the strength from Christ gave him the ability to do all things within the confines of the will of God for his life.

The underlying truth, not overtly stated in Paul's statement, is that Jesus Christ will not strengthen a person to do something He has not authorized them to do. In essence, Philippians 4:13 can be restated to say, "I can do all things through Christ who authorizes and, therefore, strengthens me to do." Your faith will suffer setbacks if you keep applying it to situations that will not yield results. Do you see how the devil can prompt a person to apply their faith inappropriately? The goal is to get you to a place of discouragement and disappointment, causing you to become cynical and eventually abandon your faith. I decree that the Lord will shield your faith from demonic attacks in Jesus' name.

Can it Still be Done if it is Not His Will?

The answer to this question is both yes and no. There are two sides to consider when addressing this question. I will share the three dimensions of faith to examine both aspects with you.

1. **On one side of the coin - you do not need God's help to create something.**

Many of the lasting inventions we have today were not invented by people that sought God's help. Genesis 11 tells of a group of people who decided to build a city and a tower whose top would reach the heavens. In essence, they wanted to build a city with a skyscraper in it. These people did not seek God's help; yet even God Himself knew that they would achieve their goal if they were not stopped. These people activated two of the three dimensions of faith.

The dimension of faith you are walking in will determine whose will you are seeking. It was not God's will for them to build a tower, so they did not activate the dimension of faith that leaned on God. They knew what they wanted, had the necessary tools to achieve their purpose outside of God and were therefore not expecting Him to do it for them. Sadly, some Christians have knowingly or unknowingly adopted this same self-sufficient approach.

When God punished the children of Israel by causing an enemy to destroy their land in an attempt to get them to repent, they doubled down on their rebellion and swore to rebuild even stronger (Isaiah 9:8-21). In some circumstances, we can use our human strength or even demonic assistance to achieve results God did not authorize. I advise you, however, to remain on God's side by sticking to His will and relying on His grace to achieve His will for your life.

2. On the flip side of the coin - can we apply our faith to anything and expect God to do it?

Are there certain limits to what we can apply our faith in God to do? As a faith-filled believer, can my faith cause God to do anything and everything I want Him to do? Although Mark 9:23 boldly states, *"Jesus said to him, 'If you can believe, all things are possible to him who believes"* this does not mean we can apply our faith to everything and expect God to bring it to pass. For example, you cannot apply your faith in God towards getting a married woman to fall in love with you, nor can you get someone healed when they do not want to be healed.

These two examples are clear cases where there is no agreement, either with the will of God or the recipient of the miracle. Hence, what this book refers to as "it" is the "will of God." It is only the will of God that can undoubtedly come to pass if we believe. The miraculous happens when our faith is aimed toward what we know to be God's will. Remember that the will of God is made known to us as promises. Abraham acted on the will (promise) of God and received its fulfillment in due time. When our faith in God is fully and boldly applied towards God's promises, know that no force in heaven or hell can stop the actualization of those promises.

In certain circumstances, our actions can cause God to change His mind and agree to something we want, even though it is contrary to His will. In Numbers 22, we read about the case of Balaam, the prophet. This prophet went to inquire of God when Balak sent for him to curse the Israelites. When Balaam went to God the first time, God told him not to dare to go with Balak's people. After Balak sweetened the offer and sent again for Balaam, Balaam went again to ask God if he could go. God told Balaam to go with Balak's people, but God was not pleased that Balaam came again to ask for permission after He had already made it clear what His will was the first time.

God knows our hearts and deals with us according to the motives and intentions of our hearts, not our words. For example, you may go to God in prayer to confirm your choice of a partner. If you go to God with your mind made up on what your choice is going to be, you cannot genuinely hear the perfect will of God. More often than not, the Lord will grant your heart's desires to you.

2

How Will it be Done?

By Faith

If you want your faith to keep growing, treat it like money that needs to be invested. As I mentioned earlier, in the spiritual realm, faith is the payment you make to receive valuable things in the kingdom of God. Faith is the currency of exchange in heaven, not money. The stronger your faith, the more you can receive from God. We are told in Mark 11:22-24:

"So Jesus answered and said to them, 'Have faith in God. For assuredly, I say to you, whoever says to this mountain, 'Be removed and be cast into the sea,' and does not doubt in his heart, but believes that those things he says will be done, he will have whatever he says. Therefore I say to you, whatever things you ask when you pray, believe that you receive them, and you will have them."

In the kingdom of God, we can treat faith as a key designed to provide us with access to the best that God has to offer. This faith is anchored in three dimensions, and failing to understand this, will ultimately short-circuit our faith. Often, believers are like the man who said to Jesus, *"I believe, but help my unbelief."* If you ever expressed your faith through your actions but still did not get results, one of the dimensions of faith was most likely missing. For faith to work the way God ordained it to work, all three dimensions must be in operation.

It is critical to understand the dimensions of faith if you want to develop a healthy and robust faith. If growth in all dimensions does not occur equally over time, this imbalance will lead to unhealthy faith. The only dimension that can outweigh the others without having any negative or adverse consequences is faith in God. Having faith in yourself without having faith in God or others will incite a proud and egotistical individual. Having faith in others without faith in yourself will lead to a dependent and insecure person.

Regardless, there are times in a believer's development when there will be an imbalance in their growth. We must recognize that this is understandable and to be expected, but we must ensure that we have a balanced faith in ourselves and others, while having an amplified faith in God in the long run. Hallelujah! An amplified faith in God is the most critical kind of faith needed for success in the long run.

FIRST DIMENSION OF FAITH: FAITH IN GOD

The Bible says that with God, all things are possible. This statement clearly shows that only faith in God will make ALL things possible. Faith in God is the most common dimension of faith in Christendom. For example, you need faith in God to become born again. An important principle worthy of being mentioned here is that your faith in someone or something has the potential to bring out the best in that person or thing; because faith has the innate ability to draw out the best from anything. Hence, when you put your faith in God, you will bring out the best that God has to offer you.

When it comes to faith in God, there are three levels:

1. **Believing that God can do it**
2. **Knowing that God will do it for you**
3. **Knowing that God has already done it for you**

Many people remain at the first level of faith in God because they know of God's ability to do whatever He says He will do. They have read about everything God can do and truly believe He is capable of anything and everything. Their problem lies in *not knowing* that God can do it for *them*. One way to know where you stand is to think about a testimony you heard and desired for yourself. Please pay close attention to how you responded to it. If you believe the testimony, it means that you know God is capable of doing it. If you think about it but find it difficult to believe that God can do the same for you, it means that you do not believe you deserve God's blessings.

I have met people who can lead others to get blessed but do not get blessed themselves. If you think about the testimony but cannot see yourself having it, you have not yet arrived at the third level of faith, where you know that He has already done what you desire of Him.

Our knowledge of God enhances our ability to believe what He says He will do, no matter how impossible it may initially sound. I once preached a message titled, "God's Resumé" that was born out of the revelation that to trust a person, you need to have an idea of what they have done in the past. David shared his resumé with Saul to gain his trust to face Goliath in battle. David said,

"Your servant used to keep his father's sheep, and when a lion or a bear came and took a lamb out of the flock, I went out after it and struck it, and delivered the lamb from its mouth; and when it arose against me, I caught it by its beard, and struck and killed it. Your servant has killed both lion and

bear; and this uncircumcised Philistine will be like one of them, seeing he has defied the armies of the living God." Moreover, David said, "The Lord, who delivered me from the paw of the lion and from the paw of the bear, He will deliver me from the hand of this Philistine." (1 Samuel 17:34-36)

Testimonies are powerful because you are exposed to God's resumé and see what He has accomplished in the past, and this can impact your opinion of what He will be able to do again. Remember, the word of God says that Jesus Christ is the same yesterday, today, and forever. (Hebrews 13:8).

God is the doer of great things. He is the restorer; purifier; King of kings; Lord of lords; Most High; I Am that I Am; and the All-wise and All-knowing God. If you put your trust in Him, no one can put you to shame. If you find your faith in Him is lacking, do not let that send you away from His presence. Like the father in Mark 9, tell him, *"Lord I believe but help my unbelief."* This means, *"Lord, here is the little faith I have, but please make it enough for what I desire from you."*

If God desires anything, it is for His children to approach Him in their current state. In James 4:2, Apostle James encouraged the believers to ask God for their hearts' desires. Now, I am asking you to, *"Ask and you shall be given, seek and you shall find, knock and the door shall be opened unto you."* (Matthew 7:7)

SECOND DIMENSION OF FAITH: FAITH IN OTHERS

The second dimension of faith is faith in other people. You may have heard it said that no man is an island on their own. Families, corporations, communities, and nations are built on the foundational idea that we all need people and that there is strength in collaboration. You display faith in others, for example, when you go to a doctor to receive medical advice or allow yourself to be sedated and operated on without your active participation. We trust grocery stores to sell us produce even though we are not fully aware of how it was grown. We confidently buy and eat all kinds of food, trusting that it was safely prepared.

In a typical developed nation, each aspect of the economy relies on the other with the understanding that everyone is operating in good faith, including the government, which should act as an unbiased umpire. We believe that the legal system will address anyone who breaches the trust. However, in third-world countries, this may not be the case.

From a spiritual perspective, it becomes even more interesting. In 2 Chronicles 20:20, the Bible tells us that we should believe in the Lord for us to be established while also believing in His prophets so we can prosper. You can see here that faith in God alone is not enough. We also must have faith in human beings, especially those sent by God. There are times when believers will not see God, but they will see people. There are also times when, through seeing people, they get to see God. By having faith in others, we are affirming the giftings of God in other people.

You may be wondering if this violates Jeremiah 17:5, which says, *"Cursed is he who places his trust in another man."* But have you taken your time to read the entire verse? This is what it says, *"Thus says the Lord, cursed is the man who trusts in man and makes flesh his strength, whose heart departs from the Lord."* This means that God does not have a problem with us having faith in people. Rather, God never wants us to have faith in people at the expense of our faith in Him. As long as your heart does not depart from the Lord, you are safe and not in violation of the above scripture. Ephesians 4:7-16 tells us that Jesus placed gifts in the church in the form of apostles, prophets, pastors, teachers, and evangelists, and we are expected to rely on them for our spiritual growth.

Can I shock you? There are certain things that the Holy Spirit will not teach you one-on-one, but He will expect you to learn from other people. If you find that you cannot trust people, you need to take it to God in prayer. If you believe that you are trustworthy, it makes sense to believe that there are other people out there who are also trustworthy.

I am sure you have heard it said that it takes a village to raise a child. That child can be a person, business or even your academics. God uses people and He expects us to trust them, just as we trust Him. That is why the Bible says that one can chase a thousand and two will chase ten thousand. You can become highly effective when you trust the right people.

"Now when the turn came for Esther the daughter of Abihail the uncle of Mordecai, who had taken her as his daughter, to go into the king, she requested nothing but what Hegai the king's eunuch, the custodian of the women, advised. And Esther obtained favor in the sight of all who saw her." (Esther 2:15)

The devil knows that we ought to have faith in others, the same way we have faith in God and ourselves; and therefore employs many strategies to cause us to lose faith in people. Those strategies are embodied in the diseases called gossip and slander. The essence of gossip, slander, and personality attacks is to kill a person's faith in others.

Another tool the enemy uses is disappointment, such as having wrong expectations of others. The enemy can suggest expectations we ought to have of others. These suggestions, though often logical, were not mutually agreed upon and, hence, are not met. The result of disappointment is that a person can lose faith in others, either completely or partially. Watch out for gossip, slander, personality attacks, and wrong expectations of others if you want your faith in the goodness of others to remain solid.

THIRD DIMENSION OF FAITH: FAITH IN YOURSELF

The dimension that binds your faith in God and others is having faith in yourself. Do you realize that most Christians have faith in God; some have faith in other Christians, yet only a few have faith in themselves? It is easier to believe that God can and will do something, but it is harder to believe God will do something specifically for them.

Faith in ourselves translates to boldness and confidence. Make no mistake, this is something you must build up intentionally because nothing of value comes free. God was angry with Moses at the beginning of his assignment because even though he had faith in the God speaking to him, he did not have faith in himself, and almost lost his assignment as a result.

Your lack of faith in yourself or others will eventually lead to a lack of faith in God if left unchecked. We must have faith in ourselves to take steps of faith. The Bible tells us that faith without works is dead, so without faith in yourself, you cannot accomplish the works of faith. Even hearing from God requires that you have faith in your capacity to hear from God. No one would deny that God speaks, but many believers have issues believing in their ability to hear from Him.

Self-doubt is a lack of faith in yourself. How many things have you not done because you did not trust in your ability to do it? Any time you find yourself struggling to obey divine instructions, it means that one of the dimensions of faith is lacking—especially faith in yourself. Do you know that once you become born-again and spirit-filled, you have the capacity to wage war against demonic forces? At what point will you be confident enough to walk in this reality? This is why many people get stuck following the dictates of the law in the Old Testament, as opposed to operating in obedience backed by grace (John 1:17). Whenever your faith in yourself stands alone without being connected to faith in God, the only option available will be the works of the law.

The works of the law, in this case, are self-righteous acts that will make you look and feel good but do not impress God because it is devoid of faith in Him. However, when you anchor your faith in God, you will be able to operate in grace.

Let me explain.

If you only believe that you can cast out demons after praying for six hours, then your faith in God is lacking. If you have faith in what God has said and believe that you can connect to what God has spoken and take action accordingly, you will get the results by grace. This is why the Bible says to trust in the Lord with all your heart and lean not on your understanding. We can even rephrase this scripture to say, *"have as much faith in God as possible, and have faith in yourself, but don't lean on faith in yourself alone."*

We must approach God with some faith in ourselves and once we get into His presence, we ought to leave our faith in ourselves at His feet. Approach God as a little child, not a man or woman of God. It is then that you can repeat the words of Paul when he said, *"I can do all things through Christ who strengthens me."* (Philippians 4:13) This scripture accurately sums up the connection between faith in yourself and faith in God.

Faith is tied to revelation. There is a reason why Paul said that *"the eyes of your understanding be enlightened."* He understood that there is a level in your relationship with God when your understanding of Him moves from "head knowledge" to "heart knowledge," or faith. This is what we call *revelation;* it is a moment of epiphany when your heart comes into agreement with what God is saying. This is why the Bible says that *"faith comes by hearing, and hearing the word of God."* (Romans 10:17)

It is said that the first hearing refers to your physical ears capturing what God is saying, while the second hearing refers to the hearing of your heart. The latter enables you to understand what God is communicating. For example, it is one thing to hear someone say that God loves you, but it is completely different to embrace and agree with this fact. When it comes to building our faith, we must pursue these light bulb moments when our spirit is stirred and comes into full agreement with God's promises.

3

Hindrances to Faith

Every Christian is designed to have faith that flows and grows. The ability of our faith to work and increase in response to life's situations is inherent. Just like a child learns to crawl, walk, and run, we were given a measure of faith when we were born again that is designed to grow organically as we journey through life.

Even though we can take actions to accelerate the growth of our faith (Romans 10:17), the gift of faith can also be imparted by the Holy Spirit (1 Corinthians 12:9). A Christian whose faith is not steadily growing over time is most likely to have encountered past events that have contaminated their faith foundation. Remember the words of Psalms 11:3, *"If the foundations are destroyed, what can the righteous do?"* Situations or past events can shake the foundation of our faith and delay or stop growth altogether. I will discuss a few of these faith-hindering conditions for your prayerful consideration.

Trauma

Trauma is a state a person finds themselves in due to a past harmful incident, be it physical, emotional or mental. Depending on the severity of a traumatic event, it can impact a person's body, mind, will, emotions, and eventually even their human spirit. Harmful events that lead to trauma can cause a person to have self-esteem issues, making their confidence lower than what it is supposed to be. Traumatic experiences have the power to disrupt the growth process of our faith in ourselves and others.

People who have been traumatized must realize that the incident also negatively impacted their faith. For example, it is helpful for a woman who has been sexually abused by a man to realize that the traumatic incident could cause her to fear or doubt the motives of every man, not just the man who abused her. Thus creating a lack of faith in men. Trauma has a way of manipulating our thought process to make broad generalizations to others beyond the actual perpetrator.

Unresolved past traumas from a father can cause a child to have difficulty trusting a male authority figure even though that authority figure has not given them a reason to doubt them. When a person consistently throws up immediately after eating, you can tell that the person's health is in jeopardy. Likewise, when a person finds it difficult to trust God, themself, or others, even after constant love has been shown to them, you can reasonably conclude that they are dealing with known or unknown trauma.

Trauma shatters our faith in humanity, which includes us as individuals. Trying to apply the contents of this book without dealing with your underlying trauma will seriously restrict your ability to grow your faith. Take, for example, the trauma that a little boy or girl suffered at the hands of a religious leader. Even though the individual is mentally aware that the religious leader does not represent all religious leaders, it will be very challenging for the victim and their loved ones to have faith in God as a result. Regardless of what has happened to you, remember that Jesus heals not just physical ailments but also emotional, mental, relationship, and financial issues.

I preached a series of messages on "Overcoming Trauma" that you can find on our Cornerstone Christian Church of God YouTube channel, where I explained how to identify trauma and receive lasting healing from traumatic events. I invite you to watch this message; I know it will be a blessing to you.

Slander and Misinformation

One thing that can affect our faith in God and others is misinformation. There are many reasons why God hates gossip, and this is one of them. I define gossip as the act of sharing information about people without their permission. The devil uses misinformation to damage the reputation of others, to cut them off from those they could have blessed. It is like a bad review someone leaves about a business. As a result of that deceptive review, some people may never get to interact with the company to gain an authentic experience. When you feel the urge to share negative information about others, ask yourself who you may be knowingly or unknowingly harming as a result.

Not everyone is authorized to speak on God's behalf. False or inaccurate teachings can damage a person's ability to know God the way they ought to. Similarly, not everyone is authorized to speak on your or my behalf. This is the reason why an organization's public relations team plays a very significant role in people's faith in the organization. You can have a good product but a bad image. Likewise, you can have a poor product but have a relatively good image. The world in which we live has waged war against the truth. It is getting more challenging, day by day, to know the truth, and it is difficult to see people who stand in truth. Since truth underpins faith, the impact of the assault on truth is an assault on faith.

Fake miracles, false revelations, and false accusations will lead people to a point where they may question their faith in themselves, others, and God. Don't get me wrong, some evil people out there need to be brought to justice. It is unfortunate, however, that some have maliciously directed the anger and indignation raging against perpetrators of injustice to settle personal scores with their adversaries. Some have falsely accused the innocent of rape and abuse, knowing that the public will begin to punish the individual before they are proven guilty.

Do not be a victim of slander and misinformation. Make it a point of duty to confirm truth like the Bereans in Acts 17:11. Unlike other Jews that Paul and his missionary team encountered on their journey, the Bereans were not quick to discard the message of the gospel just because some other Jews said so.

Disappointment and Offence

Another critical hindrance to faith can as a result of disappointments people have faced. In some cases, disappointments can be so deep that it leads to trauma. People can become disappointed when they have wrong expectations, and their faith may be severely damaged. An expectation is wrong when the individual cannot meet it. For example, no matter how much you love and train your dog, expecting it to speak like a human is wrong. Putting unreasonable expectations on people and even God can cause disappointment. You are not meant to avoid having expectations of people. Rather, you are to allow the Holy Spirit and the individual to show you what is a right or wrong expectation.

When you are disappointed, you are tempted to stop trying to collaborate with God or others to fulfill your destiny. You are tempted to run the race alone, which is absolutely impossible.

Disappointment can sometimes arise not because of a mistake but because you took someone's word as absolute. No matter how much reassurance a human being gives, remember that they are just human. Jeremiah rightly stated, "*Cursed is the man who trusts in man and makes flesh his strength, whose heart departs from the Lord"* (Jeremiah 17:5). In some cases, you put your faith in God, but perhaps your mistake was that you did not know God's will for that situation; therefore, you were disappointed. For example, you might have rightly believed that it was God's will to heal your mother, but you had a wrong expectation regarding the speed at which that healing would manifest, which led to disappointment.

When you are disappointed, you are also offended. You cannot be disappointed in someone without being offended by them. Offence and disappointment are so dangerous that Jesus advised those who come to the altar to worship with offence to leave the altar. He instructed them to resolve the offence before coming back to finalize their worship. If you retain offence in your heart or allow disappointment to fill your heart, your faith-building efforts will be in vain.

Whatever the case may be, as you read this book, may your heart be healed from disappointment and offence in Jesus' name.

4

How do we Build our Faith?

Testimonies

There are many ways we can grow our faith, but one primary way is by connecting with testimonies. The Bible says that *"they overcame by the blood of the lamb and by the word of their testimonies"* (Revelation 12:11). Something happens inside of us when we listen to testimonies. Deep down, we ponder that if God can do it for someone else, there is a great possibility He can do it for us too. This is why, when you hear testimonies, the enemy will attempt to sow doubt into you that would invalidate the authenticity of the testimony. The devil's biggest fear is that you would dare to believe that God does the miraculous. He is aware of God's power and abundance, and he knows that the moment you come to this revelation, he has lost the battle.

In Revelation 19:10, the Bible says that the testimony of Jesus is the spirit of prophecy. When you connect with other people's testimonies, you are prophesying over yourself. It is as if you are openly declaring to God, "Lord, I have seen You do it for Jane. I believe that You can and will do it for me also." Moreover, this is why Jesus encourages us to rejoice with those rejoicing. When you can celebrate God in the lives of your brothers and sisters, you qualify for the next celebration.

Let us look at one of the Bible's most profound examples of the power of testimonies. In the story of the woman with the issue of blood (Mark 5:21-34), the Bible never stated that the woman heard the testimony of someone touching the hem of Jesus' garment. She was inspired by faith to do so and received her miracle by doing something no one else did. However, throughout the Bible, her testimony spread like wildfire. By Mark 6:56, you see that anywhere Jesus went after that interaction, people were desperate to touch His garments to receive healing. The faith in the woman's heart spread into the hearts and minds of many others. Many began to imagine that *"Jesus does not even need to touch me or know that I am there for me to be healed."*

Testimonies are a very powerful way to supercharge your faith, especially when they are from people you know and you have seen their testimony manifested. Here at Cornerstone, many testimonies are being birthed due to someone else's testimony. For example, we had someone whose back was supernaturally healed after I prayed for him while meeting at a cafe. Many others heard this testimony, and it spurred their faith to receive their healing.

Anointed Messages

Another way you can build your faith is by listening to anointed messages. The Bible talks about the eunuch that was reading the book of Isaiah but had no understanding of what he was reading. God had a plan for this man. It was in God's heart to use him to spread the gospel in Ethiopia through the eunuch.

To accomplish this plan, God sent Philip to join the eunuch and his chariot. When Philip met the eunuch, he asked, "Do you understand what it is you are reading?" The eunuch replied, "How would I understand unless someone explains it to me?" The eunuch invited Philip into the chariot, and Philip began to explain Isaiah 53 to him. I believe Philip's teachings deeply moved the eunuch; this is why the eunuch's eagerness to be baptized immediately after was no surprise.

Anointed messages carry the anointing to move people to act in faith. Philip was an anointed messenger sent by God who could communicate the truth of the gospel to the eunuch. As a result, the eunuch's heart was filled with faith in Christ. Faith can also be built from the messages we read. Jesus was in the temple reading the word of God when His Spirit stirred, and He declared over Himself, "The Spirit of the Lord is upon me. He has anointed me to preach the gospel to the sick." Faith was building up in His heart regarding His identity as the Messiah.

Faith comes by hearing and can also be lost by hearing. If you are used to listening and exposing yourself to all kinds of people, you need to be very careful. Not every message delivered by a "man of God" is anointed by God. Imagine the damage that can be done to your faith by listening to someone you genuinely respect question God's ability. The faith you have built can be lost faster than you can blink by hearing a word that does not align with what the Spirit of God is saying.

Association

Faith can also be built by association. Scripture tells us that "iron sharpens iron." Who you keep closest to you matters. I am not speaking about your acquaintances. I am talking about those who have your heart—those you have given your ear. The Bible emphasizes that we ought to *"guard our hearts with all diligence, for out of it flow the issues of life."* (Proverbs 4:23) If you open your heart to someone, you have to understand that your life will begin to reflect the direction they are going.

Now, let us examine when Angel Gabriel appeared to Mary to tell her she would give birth to the saviour of the world. Mary was confused, so she questioned its possibility, mainly because she had never known a man before. In his conversation with Mary, the Angel said something very critical. He realized that Mary needed extra encouragement and faith to see this through. He told her that she should visit her cousin Elizabeth, who was once old and barren but now with a child. In essence, the Angel was telling her that to build her faith in the news she received, she needed to connect with her cousin and see what God had done for Elizabeth.

The moment Mary stepped into the same room as Elizabeth, the baby in Elizabeth's womb leaped. Faith-filled Mary's heart as these events took place, and she no longer needed confirmation. Her spirit had come into agreement with the word she received.

Beloved, this is how enriching it can be to be surrounded by faith-filled people. People who are not trying to drown your faith but are validating the faithfulness of God as you share what God is saying. We build our spiritual muscle of faith when we surround ourselves with people like Elizabeth.

In Romans 10:17, the Bible says that faith comes from hearing the word of God. When God speaks to you, and you meditate on it, your faith receives a boost. There is something about the voice of God that is very soothing, energizing, and encouraging. Remember, the Bible also says that God's commandments are not grievous. I believe this is because when God gives a command, He also provides the grace to obey that command. However, we still have a choice.

In Genesis 1, God said, *"Let there be light."* Do you know what actually created that light? Jesus Christ shed insight in John 6:63 when He said, *"The words that I speak to you are spirit and life."* The words that come from God carry the full measure of the Holy Spirit, which brings life. The more you meditate on the word of God, the more your faith grows. You must also approach the word of God with the utmost reverence and humility. Know that God's word is superior to you and is more intellectually sound than your understanding.

5

Evidence of Faith

Faith can be proven by the actions taken and the words spoken. Paul was preaching in Acts 14:9 and noticed that there was a particular crippled man who was listening very intently. Immediately, Paul saw that the man had enough faith to be healed, so he commanded him to stand up. Is it possible to tell when you have enough faith to trust in God? The simple answer is yes. Let us examine this below.

Action

The bible helps us to understand that we can identify things by their fruit (Matthew 7:16). You do not need to go looking for faith. It can be seen by your actions. This means that you do not need to fake your faith. Keep soaking in the word, and in due time, you will see yourself taking steps that show that you believe what God has said to you. I always wondered how some people were able to take certain steps of faith while I struggled to take one step until I realized how simple the process of faith-building was. You do not have to wonder how to urinate often. Just keep drinking lots of water, and you will find yourself running to the bathroom.

The woman with the issue of blood heard about Jesus and all He could do. She convinced herself that all she needed to do was touch the hem of His garment. Not only did this courageous woman think about touching the hem of Jesus' garment, she actually touched it. (Matthew 9:20-21) When your faith is complete, and you trust in God, the right action will be inevitable.

Remember that faith without works is dead. (James 2:20) Do not be in a hurry to take action and fall flat on your face. When your faith is strong, the right, sustainable actions will naturally follow. I have seen many frustrated Christians operate like a child trying so hard to walk but fall instead. They look at others performing seamlessly and miss the fact that the faith to operate flawlessly has to be built up over time. The earlier you start building your faith, the better it is for you. Soon, others will look at you and wonder why you are able to take bold steps without being fazed in Jesus' name.

Speech

Another way to know if faith is present is by listening to your words. Kenneth Hagin Sr. famously said that a person could be understood by their words. You know how much money you have by looking at your bank account. Similarly, you can tell how much faith you have by paying attention to your words, especially when you are alone and not trying to impress anyone. You can tell what a person ate, to a certain degree, from the waste they passed out. Likewise, you can tell if you have faith by the words that come out of you.

Remember, out of the abundance of the heart, the mouth speaks. (Matthew 12:34) Likewise, 2 Corinthians 4:13 states, *"And since we have the same spirit of faith, according to what is written, "I believed and therefore I spoke," we also believe and therefore speak,"* Believing always leads to speaking and continuous speaking is evidence of belief in the heart.

Since faith is a virtue that the Holy Spirit supplies, the fruit of the Spirit should be evident in someone who claims to have faith. The Bible tells us that the fruit of the Spirit is love and joy, for example. When faith comes alive, the eyes of your understanding come alive.

Our actions are a reflection of what we truly believe and what comes out of our mouths can influence what we do. So in many cases, your actions and speech work together synergistically as evidence of faith.

6

Faith in Action

Moses and the Red Sea

This is one of the most sensational miracles in the Bible; so much so, that I am certain you may have even imagined yourself parting the Red Sea. If you have not, I sure have. Let us take a closer look at this account.

After Moses negotiated the release of the children of Israel from Pharaoh's stranglehold, they assumed they were homebound. The children were shocked to realize that they were caught between a rock and a hard place after realizing that Pharaoh and his army were pursuing them from behind, while the Red Sea was ahead of them, making matters even worse.

Speaking with faith, Moses responded to the murmurings of the children of Israel. *"And Moses said to the people, 'Do not be afraid. Stand still, and see the salvation of the Lord, which He will accomplish for you today. For the Egyptians whom you see today, you shall see again no more forever. The Lord will fight for you, and you shall hold your peace.'"* (Exodus 14:13-14)

You must remember that Moses made this statement of faith before the Red Sea was parted. At this point, Moses had no idea how God was going to deliver them from the Egyptians. Still, he knew that the same God who delivered them from slavery in Egypt was the same God that would deliver them from this seemingly impossible situation.

After Moses encouraged the Israelites, the word of God came to him, and he was told to lift his rod and stretch out his hand over the sea. It was not Moses' idea that the middle of the Red Sea would be their escape route; it was God's idea.

"And the Lord said to Moses, "Why do you cry to Me? Tell the children of Israel to go forward. But lift up your rod, and stretch out your hand over the sea and divide it. And the children of Israel shall go on dry ground through thze midst of the sea." (Exodus 14:15-16)

In this case, Moses demonstrated his faith by acting on God's instructions. Moses did not demonstrate great faith by coming up with the idea to part the Red Sea; he demonstrated great faith by lifting his rod and stretching his hand over the sea. If Moses had not heard from God to ascertain His will, I can only imagine what the end result would have been.

Regardless of the situation, instead of panicking and taking irrational steps, discipline yourself to find God's will and act on it. This will produce a result similar to the result Moses obtained.

Gideon's Historic 300-Man Battle

Gideon accomplished a feat that even the famed Navy Seals would find noteworthy. Without sophisticated weapons at their disposal, Gideon led an army of 300 people to defeat an enemy too numerous to number.

"Now the Midianites and Amalekites, all the people of the East, were lying in the valley as numerous as locusts; and their camels were without number, as the sand by the seashore in multitude." (Judges 7:12)

Gideon started the expedition with 32,000 soldiers, but by the time God completed His screening, there were only 300 men remaining. The screening was not Gideon's idea. He was not the one who decided to set a world record by fighting with a small number of soldiers.

"And the Lord said to Gideon, 'The people who are with you are too many for Me to give the Midianites into their hands, lest Israel claim glory for itself against Me, saying, 'My own hand has saved me.' Now, therefore, proclaim in the hearing of the people, saying, 'Whoever is fearful and afraid, let him turn and depart at once from Mount Gilead.'" And twenty-two thousand of the people returned, and ten thousand remained. But the Lord said to Gideon, 'The people are still too many; bring them down to the water, and I will test them for you there. Then it will be, that of whom I say to you, 'This one shall go with you,' the same shall go with you; and of whomever, I say to you, 'This one shall not go with you,' the same shall not go.' So he brought the people down to the water. And the Lord said to Gideon, 'Everyone who laps from the water with his tongue, as a dog laps, you shall set apart by himself; likewise everyone who gets down on his knees to drink.' And the number of those who lapped, putting their hand to their mouth, was three hundred men; but all the rest of the people got down on their knees to drink water. Then the Lord said to Gideon, 'By the three hundred men who lapped I will save you, and deliver the Midianites into your hand. Let all the other people go, every man to his place.'" (Judges 7:2-7)

Acting according to God's will is faith while acting according to your ideas is presumption. While God has promised to respond to our faith, He never made any promises to respond to presumption. If, for instance, King Jehoshaphat (2 Chronicles 20) had read about what Gideon did and decided to do the same without God endorsing it, he would have lost the battle.

From this biblical account, it is clear that all the steps Gideon took were in response to God's instructions. Gideon was not driven by selfish ambition, jealousy or envy but by his desire to obey God. His natural response to God's instructions has made him a case study for students of faith to learn.

Mary and the Birth of Christ

Mary, the earthly mother of Jesus Christ, experienced what was, and still is, unknown to man. She conceived a child without the direct or indirect involvement of a man. God broke the rules of procreation when the Holy Spirit played the role of a man by "overshadowing" Mary for Christ to be conceived.

Mary never imagined, desired or dreamed that she would conceive a child without a man being involved. The whole idea came about when Angel Gabriel visited her. She was so puzzled that she asked the angel, "How can this be since I do not know a man?" (Luke 1:34) Angel Gabriel explained that the Holy Spirit will come upon her, and the power of the Highest will overshadow her. (Luke 1:35)

You can fast, pray, apply all the faith in heaven and on the earth, and ask God to have the Holy Spirit overshadow you to give you miraculous birth. But that kind of request will never be granted. It came to pass in Mary's life because she believed the message she was given. In other words, she accepted and believed in the will of God, as relayed by Angel Gabriel.

"Then Mary said, 'Behold the maidservant of the Lord! Let it be to me according to your word.' And the angel departed from her." (Luke 1:38)

Did you notice in the above scripture that Mary said, *"Let it be to me according to your word"*? This is the focus of faith. The focus of faith has to be the will of God, as expressed in the written or revealed word of God. In essence, Mary was saying, "It can be done."

In all these examples, the miraculous events occurred because someone believed the Will of God that was communicated to them. It is okay to exercise your faith based on your desires, but you must remember that it will not come to pass when it clashes with God's purpose.

Even in situations where you exercise your faith based on God's will, your desired timing may not be in alignment with God's will, and you may experience delays. For example, it is God's will for a man or woman to be married, but God did not say, in His word, that they will be married at a particular age or immediately after they graduate from college. While you can exercise your faith to be married at a specific age or time, God has the ultimate say to either honour that timing or not. God will eternally honour that everyone who desires to be married will be married at some point in their lifetime.

7

Who Will do it?

Our Part

Say this aloud: "I am responsible for building my faith." Jesus has given each and every one of us a measure of faith, and it is our job to take that measure of faith, however large or small and put it to work. Imagine giving someone a million dollars and then hearing that the same person, who is now a million dollars richer, complaining about lacking material things they can now afford. I can tell you, I would be a little concerned about that person. Similarly, can you imagine someone who has already been given a measure of faith complaining that they lack faith instead of increasing what they have already been given? Faith is not just a gift. It is a valuable currency we have been freely given by God.

The Bible says that Jesus is the author and finisher of our faith. He is the one who began a work of faith in us and will be the one to finish it. However, between the beginning and the end of our faith is our responsibility to apply our God-given faith on a daily basis. From the very beginning, God has partnered and communicated with man—his treasured creation. God has and will always need to partner with man to bring His desires to pass on the earth.

Like a relay race, where the success of the race is dependent on each runner, God needs a man to pull his weight for His vision to come to pass on the earth. Most of the time, we fail to see the fulfillment of a prophetic word because we do not uphold our end of the partnership. It is impossible to reach maturity in faith by doing nothing. Growing in faith is our responsibility! Invest in the currency of faith you have been given. You will only get as much out of your investment as you put in.

SET A TARGET

The first step to making this investment is to set the faith target! The faith target is your objective, which outlines the specific area you desire your faith to grow. The target will vary based on where you are in life. For example, in one season, your faith target may be to build your faith for healing, whereas, in another season, it may be to build your faith for a financial breakthrough. A faith target is something that you want to use your faith to accomplish. Just like you can save money to buy a house, you can also accumulate enough faith to attain something.

WORK HARD

Hard work is important if you want to see the will of God come to pass in your life. God worked morning and evening when creating the heavens and the earth, and He expects us to do the same. Jesus worked the same schedule, according to John 5:17. He stated, *"My Father has been working until now, and I have been working."* Do you enjoy work, or are you someone who only thanks God for Friday and not every other day of the workweek?

While hard work is good, it is not the end. We must also work smart. Smart work is the result of hard work plus the application of wisdom. Hard work is directed towards the appropriate result to ensure you are not beating the air.

OBEDIENCE

The next step is to walk in obedience. This requires you to follow every direct or indirect instruction God gives you. Obedience is what we need to be able to respond to God accordingly and can also be seen as an act of faith. It pleases God when we walk in agreement with His instruction and direction. Faith and obedience must go hand in hand if we are going to please our Heavenly Father. Hebrews 11:6 declares emphatically, *"But without faith it is impossible to please Him, for he who comes to God must believe that He is, and that He is a rewarder of those who diligently seek Him."*

Do you have faith in God? Are you able to respond to His instructions and leadings by emphatically saying, "It can be done," or do you find it difficult to believe what God says to you? Are you following God's lead or your own? Elijah was a man that obeyed God and followed His lead at all times.

"And it will be that you shall drink from the brook, and I have commanded the ravens to feed you there. So he went and did according to the word of the LORD, for he went and stayed by the Brook Cherith, which flows into the Jordan." (1 Kings 17:4-5)

Elijah could have given up on God, but he chose to walk in faith and obedience and followed where God was leading him. As a result, he experienced the abundance of God even in a dry season. In Elijah's "dry season," God chose to demonstrate His power through the use of ravens, and He can use any means to do the same in your life. However, obedience is required.

HUMILITY

Everything good has counterfeit expressions, and humility is not an exception. Genuine humility is characterized in the passage from

Philippians 2:1-11. This passage shows us what God sees as humility is often different from other cultures.

"Therefore if there is any consolation in Christ, if any comfort of love, if any fellowship of the Spirit, if any affection and mercy, fulfill my joy by being like-minded, having the same love, being of one accord, of one mind. Let nothing be done through selfish ambition or conceit, but in lowliness of mind let each esteem others better than himself. Let each of you look out not only for his own interests, but also for the interests of others. Let this mind be in you which was also in Christ Jesus, who, being in the form of God, did not consider it robbery to be equal with God, but made Himself of no reputation, taking the form of a bondservant, and coming in the likeness of men. And being found in appearance as a man, He humbled Himself and became obedient to the point of death, even the death of the cross. Therefore God also has highly exalted Him and given Him the name which is above every name, that at the name of Jesus every knee should bow, of those in heaven, and of those on earth, and of those under the earth, and that every tongue should confess that Jesus Christ is Lord, to the glory of God the Father." (Philippians 2:1-11)

From the above passage, you can see the characteristics of a humble heart. A humble person is loving, fellowships with others is like-minded with fellow believers, and does not nurse selfish ambition. A humble person sees the strengths of others, looks out for the interest of others, is confident in their identity, is comfortable serving others, and can receive praise and exaltation that emanates from God.

Another passage that explains what biblical humility looks like is Matthew 18:1-4. I remember spending time fasting and praying before Cornerstone started. I was specifically asking God what it took to be a giant in the kingdom of God, and I remember hearing the Holy Spirit clearly say, "Matthew 18:1-4."

At that time the disciples came to Jesus, saying, "Who then is greatest in the kingdom of heaven?" Then Jesus called a little child to Him, set him in the midst of them, and said, "Assuredly, I say to you, unless you are converted and become as little children, you will by no means enter the kingdom of heaven. Therefore whoever humbles himself as this little child is the greatest in the kingdom of heaven." (Matthew 18:1-4)

This scripture is validated by Numbers 12:3. Moses was recorded to be the humblest man on the face of the earth, and he became one of the most powerful prophets ever.

Humble people can be identified by the following characteristic traits:

ACCOUNTABILITY

Peter demonstrated accountability when he allowed himself to be questioned by the other disciples and apostles even though he was a leading apostle. This is a very powerful lesson for each of us. If Peter, as anointed as he was, could submit himself to scrutiny at that exalted position, we must realize that humility is the safest way to go if we want to finish strong. Genuinely making yourself accountable to the right people means that you are aware of your limitations and are ready to benefit from other people's strengths. There can never be humility unless a person has genuinely submitted their outcomes to at least one authority figure in certain areas.

Leaders, please take note that not everyone who questions you is rebellious. In Acts 11, Peter (without feeling animosity towards the disciples) took his time to explain why he was fellowshipped with the gentiles.

IDENTIFICATION

Humility is also demonstrated by your willingness and openness to being identified with a group of people. Even though Moses was not captive alongside the Israelites, he approached Pharaoh saying, "Let *my* people go." Moses identified with the people of Israel and did not consider them as just some people he was coming to rescue. They were his people. The lone ranger concept is a display of pride. It might seem rational to say that you are alone because people are wicked and untrustworthy, but if you consider yourself a good person, it is reasonable to say that there should also be at least another as good as you out there. While pride seeks to stand out at all costs, humility seeks cohesion and identity. Pride likes to be separated from others, while humility makes a person want to identify with others. Jesus identified with humankind by allowing Himself to be called the son of man. May the Holy Spirit help and empower you as you go deeper humility in Jesus' name.

CORRECTABILITY

A humble person is also correctable. The anger you feel when you are corrected signals the existence of pride and its pain. No matter how gently or lovingly you are corrected, if you feel pain or anger, it is clear that pride still exists, and it needs to be crucified. The more you subject yourself to correction, and joyfully so, the more the pride in you will die. Receiving correction will help to remind you of your mortality and how prone to mistakes you are, regardless of how much you may have tried to avoid them.

TEACHABILITY

This is another trait that is found in humble people, and has to do with how open you are to learning directly or indirectly from others. For example, Solomon displayed humility by his openness to learning even from ants (Proverbs 6:6-8). A humble person strives to learn from others and is not afraid to ask questions or ask for help when needed.

DEFENDABILITY

This component of humility measures whether the individual takes it upon themselves to defend their reputation when it is attacked. A humble person is not preoccupied with the preservation of their image from external attacks. Just like when Aaron and Mariam attacked Moses' reputation, a humble person cares less about what others think about them and would not pursue the frivolity of defending their reputation. Resist the temptation to defend your reputation. What everyone thinks about you does not matter in the grand scheme of things. All that matters is what God, you, and those you care about thinks about you.

Humility is not popular and often not comfortable. Humility is often viewed as stupidity by people who do not know better. A humble person must be confident enough to take a stand for the truth regardless of the pressure to compromise their position. We should all desire to grow these aforementioned traits. Identifying that you might be prideful is not the goal from this section. The goal for this section of the book is to encourage you to believe God for the grace to grow in humility by believing in, and practicing the insights shared here. Take your mind off the pride and focus your attention on how to grow in humility.

God's Part

The faithfulness of God is a concept that Christians need to grasp as early in their walk with God as possible. Saying God never fails is true, but even more accurate is saying God *can neve*r fail. Shadrach, Meshach, and Abednego's experience taught us that God can always be relied on to deliver His promise. When King Nebuchadnezzar commanded Shadrach, Meshach, and Abednego to be thrown into the fire for not bowing down to his golden image, the fire did not burn them. If whatever God says fails to come to pass, it means that we got it wrong or we did not play our part in the partnership. Remember, walking with God is a partnership—each partner has their own responsibilities.

OPPORTUNITIES

One of the things that God specializes in is creating opportunities. The Bible tells us in Ecclesiastes 9:11 that, *"...the race is not to the swift, nor the battle to the strong, nor bread to the wise, nor riches to men of understanding, nor favour to men of skill; but time and chance happen to them all."* Since God does not dwell in time, He is able to control time. He also does not need an opportunity because He creates opportunities.

You may be familiar with the story of Jezebel and her demonic exploits in the land of Israel, from 1 Kings 16. She was from the land of Sidon, and her father was Ethbaal, the Sidonian king. Jezebel was largely responsible for expanding the worship of Baal in Israel. She orchestrated the slaughter of the true prophets in the land of Israel and even installed her prophets of Baal to take their place.

You might not have realized that God was scheming behind the scenes. When the water dried up by the Brook of Cherith, God sent Elijah to the widow of Zarephath. Guess what? The same Zarephath belonged to Sidon. In essence, as the devil was planting Jezebel in Israel to turn their hearts away from God, God was planting Elijah in Zarephath to perform a noteworthy miracle there that would cause the name of God to be magnified. Not only that, He was going to use the same Elijah to end the worship of Baal in Israel. What is the lesson here? God has many ways to bring about a shift in a person's life.

Another example of this is Joseph. God caused Pharaoh to have a dream that none of his advisors could interpret. It just so happened that Pharaoh's chief butler was thrown into the same prison where Joseph was. Joseph had the opportunity to interpret the dream the chief butler himself had while in prison. What better interview could Joseph have had? Listen to me; God has more ways to create opportunities for His children than any other person on the face of the earth. God's job is to create the opportunity, while ours is to take full advantage of it when it arrives.

FRUITFULNESS

Have you ever thought about what makes the seeds we plant on the ground grow? Have you ever imagined what causes a man and woman to meet sexually, resulting in a child?

Solomon is famed for having said, "*...Blessed be the Lord God of Israel, who spoke with His mouth to my father David, and with His hand has fulfilled it.*" 1 Kings 8:15, God never says what He cannot do. In fact, there is nothing He is unable to do, even though there are things He will never do because of His nature, like telling a lie.

It is God who told the children of Israel to keep marching into the Red Sea because He had the ability to make a way through it. Your walk with God will be enhanced when you realize that He is not limited like humans are. He is not bound by time; He has unlimited material and emotional and mental resources. He has unlimited power, speed, and sight. Abraham was able to walk with God and demonstrate faith in God because he knew God's capabilities.

Romans 4:21 says that Abraham was fully aware of God's ability to perform what He had promised. How amazing! Remember, you give in to worry and anxiety when you stray from focusing on what you have to God's ability to play His part. Focus on your responsibilities in the God-human partnership and watch how everything God promises will come to pass.

8

When Will it be Done?

Times and Seasons

Beloved, it is time you realize that nothing you have experienced in the past or will encounter in the future is a coincidence. All seasons of life have God's fingerprints etched into them. Time and seasons are in God's hands. He orchestrates every second, minute, and hour of our lives.

Right now, where you are is a result of the season God has placed you or where you placed yourself as a result of disobedience to divine instructions. The Bible tells us that *"...the race is not to the swift, nor the battle to the strong, neither yet bread to the wise, nor yet riches to men of understanding, nor yet favour to men of skill; but time and chance happeneth to them all"* (Ecclesiastes 9:11). If swiftness, strength, wisdom, understanding, or even skill can be controlled by time and chance (opportunity), then the One who is in control must be greater than each of these manifestations.

Think of it like this. A farmer knows the right season to begin cultivating the ground for planting. He plants with the future in mind.

For each seed sown in one season, there is a time and season when the seed will begin to germinate and grow. Farmers plant with a strong sense of time and season; it is the tool that helps them reap the best crops at harvest. They control when a seed is planted and know when it flourishes. God can be likened to a farmer who plants seeds with our past, present and future in mind. In every season (for those who have come and those who will come), God provides specific tools and experiences that help shape and shift us into the next stage of our walk with Christ.

As children of God, life does not just "happen" to us. God is so intentional with His children that He ensures that life happens *for* us. In Romans 8:28, God promises to work all things out for the good of those that love Him and are called according to His purpose. This scripture should fill you with enough faith to believe that with God, there are no "ups and downs" in life. Instead, think of it as smooth sailing because you believe that even when life seemingly appears out of line, it is just a matter of time before you see God's hand in that season. Our expectation should always be that we move from glory to glory in every aspect of our lives. The Bible makes no mistake when it says that *"the path of the just is like the shining sun, that shines ever brighter unto the perfect day"* (Proverbs 4:18). Imagine yourself like an early morning sun slowly rising. As you rise, your light continues to shine brighter and brighter in every season.

Light Controls Time

The concept of time came about when God created light. This means that before God created light, there was nothing like time. There was no concept of past, present or future. How the arrival of light on the earth brought about the concept of time is the same as how the arrival of light on a person will bring about the concept of time.

"Then God said, "Let there be lights in the firmament of the heavens to divide the day from the night; and let them be for signs and seasons, and for days and years; and let them be for lights in the firmament of the heavens to give light on the earth"; and it was so. Then God made two great lights: the greater light to rule the day, and the lesser light to rule the night. He made the stars also. God set them in the firmament of the heavens to give light on the earth, and to rule over the day and over the night, and to divide the light from the darkness. And God saw that it was good. So the evening and the morning were the fourth day." (Genesis 1:14-19)

From Genesis 1:14-19, we can see that light was created to do the following:

1. **To divide the day from the night**
2. **To be for signs**
3. **To be for seasons**
4. **To mark the days**
5. **To mark the years**
6. **To divide light from darkness**

Let me explain the last point above. The light-emitting bodies that God created - the sun, moon, and stars - are able to divide enlightened from unenlightened people. So, the focus or lack of focus of the light from the sun, moon, or stars upon a person can cause there to be light or darkness upon them. I implore you to think about that for a moment.

Once a person becomes enlightened, they will become aware of the movement of time and their need to make the best use of it. In like manner, darkness is associated with the wastage of time. A person under the oppression of depression or heaviness typically loses track of time. In contrast, a person operating in the grace of God is typically able to make the best use of time.

As you see the relationship between light and time, you will now realize that the one who controls light will also control time. The one who controls enlightenment will control timeliness. What you make of your time on earth is directly proportional to the amount of light in, on and around you. It is scientifically proven that the faster you get to the speed of light, the slower you will seem to those operating at a slower pace. So, the brighter the faster; and the darker the slower.

To be enlightened is to have light in you. The moment this happens, you are now able to determine your own rhythms as you go through life. You become a custodian of times and seasons. One of the most powerful books I have written thus far is The Enlightened Believer. It is short, unassuming, but with powerful atomic revelations that can bring about seismic shifts in a person's life.

To be favoured, honoured or loved is to have light upon you. This is what happens when God makes you the center of attraction. Remember Psalms 102:13, *"You will arise and have mercy on Zion; for the time to favour her, yes, the set time, has come."* When light comes upon you, it is time for you to be favoured, honoured, and loved. Also, remember Isaiah 60:1-3,

Arise, shine; for your light has come! And the glory of the Lord is risen upon you. For behold, the darkness shall cover the earth, and deep darkness the people; But the Lord will arise over you, and His glory will be seen upon you. The Gentiles shall come to your light, and kings to the brightness of your rising.

Finally, to have light around you means to surround yourself with light-emitting individuals and institutions. The light in and on you is not enough to take you to the top and keep you from falling. You have to surround yourself with other enlightened individuals so you are able to also benefit from their light. It is then that you now begin to enjoy the provisions of Proverbs 27:17, *"As iron sharpens iron, so a man sharpens the countenance of his friend."* Jesus started with light in Him before the light came upon Him, and eventually, He surrounded Himself with disciples who now also had the light of Christ upon them.

Fullness of Time

There is a thin line between taking steps of faith to pre-empt the move of God and waiting on God's perfect time. It is good to have your faith targeted towards a goal, but it becomes an issue when you expect God to act according to your desired timing. God is not obligated to do things at our command, and the times He does, it is most likely because He already had it planned that way. It is a huge mistake to think we can force the hand of God to do anything. God reserves the right to move in His own time. Romans 2:11 makes it very clear that God is no respecter of man. When you do not know the timing God has for you in a given season, that is when you begin to exercise your faith to firmly believe that it will indeed happen in God's appointed time.

For instance, even though children are a heritage from the Lord (Psalms 127:3), the Bible never says when God will release children into a marriage. Some couples can have children immediately after getting married, while others can receive this blessing after five years. Like Sarah and Elizabeth, some people may even have their children in their old age. In the same vein, even though it is God's will that a man should not be alone (Genesis 2:18) and should be joined to a woman in marriage, God never specified when this must happen. For some, marriage will happen in their 20s, some in their 30s, and some even in their 50s. Our God is a God of times and seasons. Many scriptures talk about God's timing. Here are a few of them:

"You will arise and have mercy on Zion; For the time to favour her, yes, the set time, has come." (Psalms 102:13)

"But when the fullness of the time had come, God sent forth His Son, born of a woman, born under the law, to redeem those who were under the law, that we might receive the adoption as sons." (Galatians 4:4-5)

"He has made everything beautiful in its time. Also He has put eternity in their hearts, except that no one can find out the work that God does from beginning to end." (Ecclesiastes 3:11)

"For He says: In an acceptable time I have heard you, and on the day of salvation I have helped you." Behold, now is the accepted time; behold, now is the day of salvation." (2 Corinthians 6:2)

"But of that day and hour no one knows, not even the angels in heaven, nor the Son, but only the Father." (Mark 13:32)

"I said in my heart, "God shall judge the righteous and the wicked, for there is a time there for every purpose and for every work." (Ecclesiastes 3:17)

"Thus says the Lord: "In an acceptable time I have heard You, and in the day of salvation I have helped You; I will preserve You and give You as a covenant to the people, to restore the earth, to cause them to inherit the desolate heritages..." (Isaiah 49:8)

God's timing for everything is impeccable. *"But when the fullness of the time had come, God sent forth His Son, born of a woman, born under the law, to redeem those who were under the law, that we might receive the adoption as sons"* (Galatians 4:4-5). Jesus Christ was born when the fullness of time had come. In line with His birth, it means that John the Baptist, being His forerunner, also had to be born at a specific time. God had ordained that John the Baptist would be born into the household of Zachariah and Elizabeth. This significant event meant that no amount of prayer would have enabled them to have children before the appointed time.

Many Christians are mistakenly frustrated with God because they lack understanding of His way and time of doing things. Often, they focus their attention on how they feel. Once you view the fulfillment of prophecy through the lens of God's purpose, it will become easier for you to understand God's perfect timing. Martha was disappointed in Jesus Christ because she did not see the will of God in the death of her brother, Lazarus, and the arrival of Jesus. A believer can become disappointed and lose their faith. We understand from Proverbs 13:12 that *"hope deferred makes the heart sick, but when the desire comes, it is a tree of life."* Even though God has every intention to grant us our desires, His primary focus is the fulfillment of His purpose. In the example of Lazarus, God's purpose was for Lazarus to die and be raised back to life after four days. This resurrection would cause many to believe in Jesus and be saved as a result.

How to Understand Times and Seasons

Among the men in David's army was a group of men known as the sons of Issachar. These men had a clear understanding of the times. In every season, they had insight into the direction Israel was to move. For you and me, such knowledge can only come from the ministry of the Holy Spirit.

In speaking about the Holy Spirit, Jesus said, *"However, when He, the Spirit of truth, has come, He will guide you into all truth; for He will not speak on His own authority, but whatever He hears He will speak; and He will tell you things to come"* (John 16:13). Part of the ministry of the Holy Ghost is to help us realize the specific season God has us in and guide us through it. He is the one that brings clarity and understanding of what God is doing in and around us in real-time. If you are curious about what God is doing, get in touch with His personal assistant, the Holy Spirit!

Mark 11:23 is a scripture I use as a yardstick when exercising my faith concerning the desires I entrust to God. This scripture helps keep my heart in check. Over the years, I have learned to check my heart when something I have earnestly requested from God is not taking shape. I always want to ensure that I am in the right standing before God. When my heart is clear in that area, I spend time communing with the Holy Spirit to find out if the timing I had in mind clashes with what God has ordained. In my case, the Holy Spirit confirms that my request is in line with the will of God; however, God's plan sets the timing. Knowledge like this sets my mind at rest, as I know the promise will come to pass in due season. My faith is nourished, and my trust in God is protected because of His faithfulness.

Another way to understand times and seasons is by discernment. In Luke 12:54-56, Jesus scolded the multitudes for being able to observe the change in the weather but not being able to discern time.

"Then He also said to the multitudes, "Whenever you see a cloud rising out of the west, immediately you say, 'A shower is coming'; and so it is. And when you see the south wind blow, you say, 'There will be hot weather'; and there is. Hypocrites! You can discern the face of the sky and of the earth, but how is it you do not discern this time?"

No one in the audience was filled with the Holy Spirit, so Jesus could not have asked them to follow the Holy Spirit's lead. The example Jesus gave was appropriate because anyone should be able to look up at the sky and know what is happening with the weather by observation. If Jesus corrected the multitude for not discerning the time, it means that we can indeed discern times and seasons.

God programmed the earth based on times and seasons. We see in Ecclesiastes 3:1-2 that *"To everything there is a season, A time for every purpose under heaven: A time to be born, And a time to die; A time to plant, And a time to pluck what is planted"* The children of God are expected to understand times and seasons so we are able to make the best use of each day.

Learning to observe patterns and cycles can help us grow in wisdom. For example, you may notice that people are suddenly coming to give you a particular gift, like food. It is no longer a coincidence that, daily, someone has been coming to buy you food for the past two weeks. If you do not take your time to observe this pattern, you can miss the season in which you find yourself. These were Solomon's thoughts in Ecclesiastes 3. He was imploring us to understand life's different patterns and cycles.

Adjust Your Focus

As believers, we must familiarize ourselves with the concept of sowing and reaping. If you can understand this principle, I guarantee you will reap benefits in every season of life.

Seasons of sowing can easily be mistaken for downtime—when things are quiet, seemingly uneventful on God's end and life's challenges are at an all-time high. Times of harvest can also be misunderstood as peak seasons of celebration. Sadly, many people do not realize that sowing seasons are foundational to all the good things we enjoy at harvest. Many people waste their sowing seasons, complaining or bearing malice towards God as if He has abandoned them. Can you imagine if farmers wasted planting seasons this way? People fail to see that God is in every season and has a purpose for every season. Our Heavenly Father is Lord over all seasons, hallelujah!

In seasons of sowing, the real intentions of our hearts are exposed. We begin to walk in troubled waters when we misuse the purpose of our sowing seasons. It is naturally not fun to be in the sowing season. Everything around you becomes a reflection of what you desire but do not yet have. You start seeing everyone else around you at ease, diligently running their race, sowing all kinds of seeds, while you are still focusing on how things are not working for you. Child of God, I have good news; this will not happen to you, in Jesus' name!

When you connect to times of sowing and embrace its hustle, you will quickly realize that no matter what season you are in, God has your back. Look at Abraham, Isaac, and Joseph, for example. Even in times of famine, Jehovah Jireh made provisions for His children. These men continued to be obedient and diligent in their service to God, and God made sure their cups never ran dry.

The perspective you take during times of sowing and reaping is directly related to what you get out of it, and I am not just talking about material things. When you complain and drag your feet through any season God has you in, you forfeit more than just material blessings; you forfeit growth. Essentially, you are saying to God, "In this season, I want to remain the same."

You might say, "Pastor, why do bad things still happen to me, even when I sow when I am supposed to?" The answer to this question is tied back to the perspective you take when you are in a sowing season. When it is sowing time, you may battle with discouragement, disappointment, and maybe even depression. It may seem as though God has forgotten about you. If you keep your eyes on God, you will see that God is good every season. You will see how intentional He is about where He has you.

I want you to ask yourself, "What season am I in right now?" Begin to think about the possibilities God could be cultivating for you. The beauty of times and seasons is that we are never all in the same season. There are always differences that distinguish us from each other. Even in the body of Christ, we are all in different growing seasons. As the Lead Pastor of Cornerstone, I can tell you that the season we are in as a church today is not the same season we will be in down the road. God is moving in Cornerstone according to His ordained time for us, and it is beautiful.

Never Stop Sowing

The key to transitioning from one season to another is to never stop sowing! The Bible teaches us this in Psalm 126:6, where it says, *"He who continually goes forth weeping, bearing seed for sowing, shall doubtless come again with rejoicing, bringing his sheaves with him."* Child of God, whether you find yourself on a mountain top or in a valley, continue to pour out and sow in each season because a time is coming when you will see the fruits of your efforts. Rest assured, it will come, and the joy that will overflow in your heart will spur the whole process again.

If you are not sowing, you cannot expect to reap. It is a cause-and-effect relationship. You will always reap what you sow, so the key is to never stop sowing!

Joseph understood this concept quite well. While many of his peers were improving and being promoted, Joseph kept his head in the trenches. He knew the season he was in and was focused on preparing for what he was expecting to see in his future. I am sure people questioned his behaviour, wondering if something was wrong with him.

Even in Potiphar's house, he continued to sow seeds. He continued to add value until one day, the spotlight of favour dawned on him, and everyone who never expected anything to come from Joseph's life was confused. They did not know that he was sowing all along; it was only a matter of time before he transitioned to a season of a bountiful harvest.

Add Value

Let us shift gears a little here and talk about the substance of the seeds you are sowing. Many people mistake sowing seeds as just a monetary "gift" to God, which it can be if your intention is to appreciate God. However, it is equally important to understand that the art of sowing is much greater than money.

In fact, God is not just looking at the replaceable material items you can give. He is also looking at the sacrifices you are willing to make. What am I saying here? I am saying God wants you to occasionally *give up* things instead of simply giving Him things. Giving money to God or a spiritual authority is wonderful, but my question is, are you also able to give up your time or sleep in a season where God wants to draw you in closer to Him? The substance of your seed is measured by how valuable it is to you and to God.

While you are waiting for the fulfillment of God's promises to you, what are you doing? You can continue to sow by adding value to those around you. Take the focus off of yourself and search for areas in your family, school, work, and the church where you can add value. Personally, I avoid idleness because it leads to temptations of comparison, jealousy, envy, and other heart-related sinful thoughts and behaviours. When you focus on your God-given purpose, you will not realize how much time has gone by since you asked God for something and when He delivered it.

Have you realized that when you are twiddling your thumbs and watching the time it seems to be at a standstill? However, when you are productively engaged, time goes by seemingly faster. God does not tolerate people that do not add value. He is looking for hearts and hands that are committed and ready to work to see the kingdom of God move forward.

As a Pastor, people sometimes assume that the church takes advantage of members not currently working by giving them work to do in the ministry. However, they do not realize that people can add value even if they are not currently in a paid position. God has given each of us gifts. Giving back to Him what He has blessed us with is more than enough. Everything God has made is designed to add value, including you! You will eventually be paid by God for the value you are genuinely adding today.

John 15:1-2 says, *"I am the true vine, and my Father is the vinedresser. Every branch in Me that does not bear fruit He takes away; and every branch that bears fruit He prunes, that it may bear more fruit."* In other words, if you are not functioning at the capacity God has given to you, you are not useful in God's hands. It sounds harsh, but my friend, it is the truth.

It is like going to the store and purchasing a product that has been advertised to perform a specific task. When you now use the product, it does not work as it should. Your two options are to replace it with one that works or get rid of the whole product. With God, the decision is to get rid of the whole product!

Use Your Words to Sow The Right Seeds

Words are powerful! They can build a person up, or they can destroy a person. How and when words are used is subject to the individual. When it comes to sowing, the use of our words is another way we can plant seeds.

Imagine the frustration you would feel after sowing all your seeds, only to realize that there is no harvest because of your spoken words. You become your own devourer when the declarations you make over yourself contradict the actions you take to experience blessings. It is like adding and then immediately subtracting from your life. Blessing and then cursing yourself.

The reality of this cycle is heartbreaking because of how often and how easily we do this. Imagine a mother with children she loves dearly. Day in and day out, she prays that God will draw her children to salvation, but from the same lips, she pours out curses towards them. Do you think her prayer to save her children will still be effective? No. She voided the prayers using her mouth.

I want you to really understand how detrimental it can be to your spiritual growth when you speak negative words about yourself or a situation and expect good returns. You are hindering the growth of your faith every time you make contradictory declarations! The devil will use it as an opportunity to suggest to you that God is not good and that He does not respond to your prayers. God does respond, but He cannot agree with you concerning the things you have already spoken against and voided. Sometimes, this is how disappointment and discouragement are birthed, but the good news is you have now identified one of the root causes. The children of Israel did not understand this, but God helped them understand quickly.

"Now when the people complained, it displeased the Lord; for the Lord heard it, and His anger was aroused. So the fire of the Lord burned among them, and consumed some in the outskirts of the camp" (Numbers 11:1). I can picture how displeased God might have been to have to show up

the way He did. I think it is safe to say that part of the reason the children of Israel were strung out in the desert for so long was because of the words they were speaking, even after receiving such a great promise from God.

Child of God, you can end the cycle by beginning to sow declarations of life and faith into every season! You are in control of what you say, and when you say it, so speak with boldness, wisdom, and faith!

"Walk prudently when you go to the house of God; and draw near to hear rather than to give the sacrifice of fools, for they do not know that they do evil. Do not be rash with your mouth, And let not your heart utter anything hastily before God. For God is in heaven, and you on earth; Therefore, let your words be few. For a dream comes through much activity, And a fool's voice is known by his many words. When you make a vow to God, do not delay to pay it; For He has no pleasure in fools. Pay what you have vowed— Better not to vow than to vow and not pay. Do not let your mouth cause your flesh to sin, nor say before the messenger of God that it was an error. Why should God be angry at your excuse and destroy the work of your hands? For in the multitude of dreams and many words there is also vanity. But fear God." (Ecclesiastes 5:1-7)

Anything you would never want to see in or around you should never come out of your mouth. If it is a great harvest you are expecting to see, speak the harvest into existence while waiting for it to happen. Create the reality you hope to see with your words and watch your faith grow every step of the way.

9

The Spirit of Faith

As we discussed earlier, there are different types of faith. In this section, we will explore the spirit of faith. You can understand it this way. The other kinds of faith are based on human principles; however, the spirit of faith operates in a different way. According to 1 Corinthians 12, the Holy Spirit can supply faith as one of His gifts and is known as the spirit of faith.

Let us remind ourselves of a few things. A person can exist in different realms. There is the earthly realm and the spiritual realm. The earthly realm operates based on earthly principles and is subject to earthly limitations. The spiritual realm is different. Most of the limitations that are experienced in the earthly realm are non-existent. Things like speed, distance, time, and weight are not applicable in the spiritual realm.

When a spiritual force is invited to operate in the earthly realm, the result is an undue advantage. Jesus was well aware of this, and it was why He told the disciples that it was in their best interest that He left, which allowed the Holy Spirit to come. Throughout human history, man has made efforts to summon spiritual forces because of the advantage they expect to receive. While different spiritual forces are available, they are not all at the same level. Unlike other religious practices, the Holy Spirit is the only spirit that does not have to be divided based on the various blessings He can offer.

When it comes to operating in faith, the Holy Spirit can enable us to believe anything God wants us to believe. 2 Corinthians 4:13 makes reference to the spirit of faith. This is significant because Paul is alluding to the fact that, when needed, the Holy Spirit has the power to cause us to supernaturally believe whatever God is instructing us to do, even to our amazement. You will know that your faith was empowered by the Holy Spirit when you look back after having obeyed God's instruction, and you realize there was no way you could have obeyed that instruction without His divine assistance.

You may be wondering, "How can I get the Holy Spirit to give me supernatural faith when needed?" The answer is in 1 Corinthians 12:11. The Holy Spirit distributes the gifts as He wills, so do your best to walk with God daily. When needed, the spirit of faith will come into operation. The spirit of God is a passageway from one realm to the other. It operates like a highway, a transportation system. Living life without operating through the spirit of faith can cause a person's journey to success to be longer and more tedious. Let us now discuss some evidence of the spirit of faith at work in a believer's life.

INSTANT SUPERNATURAL BOLDNESS

The Holy Spirit is the custodian of life. There is a reason why Jesus said it was going to be in our favour for Him to leave for the Holy Spirit to come upon all believers. One of the pieces of evidence that the spirit of faith is upon an individual is in the boldness they display. In speaking about Caleb, God alluded to "a different spirit in him" as the reason why he was able to take bold steps when the other ten spies delivered a negative report. There are many "Calebs" on the earth today because of the spirit of faith at work in them. How else will you explain the bold and audacious steps Reinhard Bonnke and his team takes every time they set out to organize large crusades on the other side of the world? Here is what God said about Caleb:

"...because all these men who have seen My glory and the signs which I did in Egypt and in the wilderness, and have put Me to the test now these ten times, and have not heeded My voice, they certainly shall not see the land of which I swore to their fathers, nor shall any of those who rejected Me see it. But My servant Caleb, because he has a different spirit in him and has followed Me fully, I will bring into the land where he went, and his descendants shall inherit it." (Numbers 14:22-24)

SUPERNATURAL ABILITY TO BELIEVE

Another aspect of the spirit of faith is that it enables us to believe anything God says, no matter the situation we face. We cannot speak about the spirit of faith without referring to Abraham, the father of faith. It is easy to believe God after seeing evidence of what He can do from His word or live testimonies. However, the spirit of faith will enable us to believe whatever it is that God says instantly.

To a degree, the individual under the influence of the spirit of faith will operate like someone who is intoxicated. How did Abraham believe God's word about having a child in his old age without any previous evidence? How was Abraham able to instantly believe God by obeying the instruction to sacrifice Isaac? How did Abraham believe God's promise to him about his descendants taking over the land of Canaan? I tell you, it is because he was under the influence of the Holy Spirit. Without knowing how Abraham could believe God to that extent, you will be frustrated in your faith life. There are times when all we need at the moment is the Holy Spirit's gift of faith. It is written in Romans 4:13-22:

"For the promise that he would be the heir of the world was not to Abraham or to his seed through the law, but through the righteousness of faith. For if

those who are of the law are heirs, faith is made void and the promise made of no effect, because the law brings about wrath; for where there is no law there is no transgression. Therefore it is of faith that it might be according to grace, so that the promise might be sure to all the seed, not only to those who are of the law, but also to those who are of the faith of Abraham, who is the father of us all (as it is written, 'I have made you a father of many nations') in the presence of Him whom he believed—God, who gives life to the dead and calls those things which do not exist as though they did; who, contrary to hope, in hope believed, so that he became the father of many nations, according to what was spoken, 'So shall your descendants be.' And not being weak in faith, he did not consider his own body, already dead (since he was about a hundred years old), and the deadness of Sarah's womb. He did not waver at the promise of God through unbelief but was strengthened in faith, giving glory to God, and being fully convinced that what He had promised He was also able to perform. And therefore 'it was accounted to him for righteousness.'"

SUPERNATURAL FAITH UTTERANCE

When the spirit of faith is at work, we will speak the right way in response to a seemingly tough situation. In 2 Corinthians 4:13, we see that the spirit of faith is a speaking spirit.

"And since we have the same spirit of faith, according to what is written, 'I believed and therefore I spoke,' we also believe and therefore speak..."(2 Corinthians 4:13)

Have you realized that when you are afraid, you are usually unable to speak or, in some cases, unable to speak coherently? The spirit of faith speaks life into every dead situation. The spirit of faith speaks of victory even when defeat seems imminent. The spirit of faith speaks of abundance when scarcity appears to be evident. The spirit of faith always gives a good report, no matter the situation.

In Numbers 13:30, we see how the spirit of faith enabled Caleb to speak differently from the other spies. After the other spies spoke fearful words of defeat, *"Caleb quieted the people before Moses and said, "Let us go up at once and take possession, for we are well able to overcome it."* However, immediately after Caleb's bold declarations, the ten spies again saturated the atmosphere with fearful words.

"But the men who had gone up with him said, 'We are not able to go up against the people, for they are stronger than we.' And they gave the children of Israel a bad report of the land which they had spied out, saying, 'The land through which we have gone as spies is a land that devours its inhabitants, and all the people whom we saw in it are men of great stature. There we saw the giants (the descendants of Anak came from the giants), and we were like grasshoppers in our own sight, and so we were in their sight." (Numbers 13:31-33)

What you say is so important that the Bible said, *"for by your words you will be justified, and by your words you will be condemned."* (Matthew 12:37)

GENERATION OF SUPERNATURAL RESULTS

The spirit of faith is at the root of every supernatural result. In the very beginning of creation in Genesis 1, the Holy Spirit—the custodian of the gift of faith—was hovering over the face of the waters before our heavenly Father began making bold declarations and formations, which resulted in this beautiful place we call earth. The operation of the spirit of faith will enable you to break new frontiers. The result of bold declarations and bold steps sponsored by the Holy Spirit is supernatural. When the gift of faith is in operation, the effect is what eyes have not seen nor entered into the heart of man. Thank you, Jesus! I see you achieving supernatural feats in Jesus' mighty name.

Too many Christians are afraid of the unknown. Dear brothers and sisters, faith is the solution. The Bible tells us that we have not been given the spirit of fear but of power, love, and a sound mind. (2 Timothy 1:7) The spirit of faith is the opposite of the spirit of fear. In essence, the solution to fear is faith. When the spirit of faith is in operation, it will seem like the recipient has already successfully performed the venture they are about to undertake. Yes, you read that right. The spirit of faith imparts supernatural experiences.

When David faced Goliath in 1 Samuel 17, it seemed as if he had previously defeated Goliath in battle. David was assured of supernatural results. When Saul sent for David, after hearing his supernatural utterances of faith, David referred to previous experiences with wild beasts as evidence that he could defeat Goliath. We both know that a lion and a bear are not human. No matter how strong or deadly those animals were, they were not at the same level as Goliath in size, battle experience, weaponry, and force. Yet, David was more than assured of his victory in the confrontation with Goliath.

The Holy Spirit is the custodian of supernatural faith. Any spiritual discipline that draws you closer to God will increase your chances of operating in the gift of faith. Like every other spiritual gift, we need to ask in order to receive. We need to seek to find. We need to knock for access to the gift to be given (Matthew 7:7). I can tell you about the importance of praying regularly in the spirit. (Jude 1:20) I can tell you about the need to walk in holiness, not to quench the spirit (Thessalonians 5:19). I can tell you about the importance of constantly fellowshipping with the Holy Spirit (2 Corinthians 13:14) and many other formulas for positioning yourself to operate in the gift of faith. However, the Bible is clear in 1 Corinthians 12:11 that the gifts of the spirit are distributed as the Holy Spirit wills. This means that the dissemination of the gift of faith is at the sole discretion of the Holy Spirit.

You can pray, fast, earnestly desire the best gift, sow seeds, and apply every other provision of scripture for receiving valuable things from God. However, we must position our hearts with the understanding that the Holy Spirit retains full discretion to give each of us the gifts He knows we need for our assignment at every point in time.

Epilogue

In this book, I have attempted to lay out the roadmap to enable you to enhance your walk of faith. However, since faith without works is dead, you will get the best from this book only when you apply its contents.

Friend, no matter the current level of your faith, taking the right steps as you have seen in this book can cause your faith to grow. As your faith grows, your love for God and humanity will grow. As your faith grows, your peace, joy, longsuffering, kindness, etc. will grow. In essence, your quality of life will grow as your faith grows.

It is true that what God cannot do does not exist, but this book was written as a roadmap to show you how to engage the power of God so your life operates at a supernatural level. Having an active and genuine faith in God, yourself, and others will drastically elevate your life. Imagine what you could do if you truly believed that every of God's promises in His word had your name on them? Imagine how much success you will have if you operated with absolute confidence that God is on your side? Imagine how much progress you will experience if you believe that those against you can never harm you? Imagine if you truly knew that you can never fall sick? Imagine if you genuinely believed that no weapon formed against you will never prosper? Friends, these and many more are possible in the realm of faith.

The realm of faith is the realm of possibilities. Faith makes the possibility of your success through life elastic. The degree to which you believe God, yourself and others is the degree to which you will succeed through life. I say to you what Jesus said to the father of the oppressed child in Mark 9:23, *"If you can believe, all things are possible to him who believes."* Go and do likewise. You have the ability to believe. Choose to believe God in all things and I can assure you that everyday will be a day of rejoicing and testimonies in Jesus' name.

Contact the Author

I know without a doubt that this book has been a blessing to you. I am looking forward to hearing your testimony.

You can contact me through email at emmanuel.adewusi@cc-cghq.org or visit emmanueladewusi.org for more information.

A Sinner's Prayer

Dear Heavenly Father,

I come to You in the Name of Jesus Christ.

You said in Your Word, "Whosoever shall call upon the name of the Lord shall be saved" (Romans 10:13). I am calling on Your Name, so I know You have saved me now.

You also said that "if you confess with your mouth the Lord Jesus and believe in your heart that God has raised Him from the dead, you will be saved. For with the heart one believes unto righteousness, and with the mouth, confession is made unto salvation" (Romans 10:9-10). I believe in my heart Jesus Christ is the Son of God. I believe that He was raised from the dead for my justification, and I confess Him now as my Lord and Savior.

Thank you, Lord, because now, I am saved!

Thank You, Lord, because I know you have heard my prayer. Thank You, Lord, because I am now born again.

Signed _____

Date _____

About the Author

Emmanuel Adewusi is the Founding and Lead Pastor of Cornerstone Christian Church Of God.

Called into ministry with the mandate to "bring restoration and transformation to all by teaching, preaching and demonstrating the gospel of Jesus Christ," he is passionate to see lives restored and transformed the way God intended from the beginning of creation. He has a passion for the full counsel of the word of God, fellowship with the Holy Spirit and being under spiritual authority.

He hosts several *"Come and See"* Conferences, with the goal to reach lost souls for Jesus Christ.

He authored the books *"Now That You Are Born Again, What Next?"*, *"The Blessings of Being Under Spiritual Authority"*, *"A Disciplined Life"*, *"Interconnected Systems: A Wisdom Manual"*, *"Channels of Grace: How to Seamlessly Connect & Stay Connected with God"*, and other impactful titles. He has also released an album titled *"Divine Encounter"* and many more on the way.

Emmanuel Adewusi is joyfully married to his wife, Ibukun Adewusi, and together, they are building a thriving Christ-centered family.

CPSIA information can be obtained
at www.ICGtesting.com
Printed in the USA
BVHW030459010822
643492BV00002B/5

9 781989 099124